It's another Quality Book from CGP

This book is for anyone doing GCSE OCR B Geography.

Whatever subject you're doing it's the same
old story — there are lots of facts and you've just got
to learn them. KS4 Geography is no different.

Happily this CGP book gives you all that important
information as clearly and concisely as possible.

It's also got some daft bits in to try and make the whole
experience at least vaguely entertaining for you.

What CGP is all about

Our sole aim here at CGP is to produce the highest quality
books — carefully written, immaculately presented and
dangerously close to being funny.

Then we work our socks off to get them out to you
— at the cheapest possible prices.

Contents

Published by CGP

Editors:
Ellen Bowness, Joe Brazier, Taissa Csaky, Chris Dennett,
Murray Hamilton, Kate Redmond, Jane Towle, Karen Wells.

Contributors:
Rosalind Browning, Paddy Gannon, Barbara Melbourne, Sophie Watkins.

Proofreading:
Glenn Rogers, Eileen Worthington.

ISBN: 978 1 84762 373 7

With thanks to Laura Phillips for copyright research.

With thanks to iStockphoto.com for permission to reproduce the photographs used on pages 7, 11, 19, 23, 40, 45, 52, 59, 60, 62, 63 and 64.

Mapping data on pages 10, 22, 103 and 104 reproduced by permission of Ordnance Survey® on behalf of HMSO © Crown copyright (2009). All rights reserved. Ordnance Survey® Licence No. 100034841.

With thanks to Science Photo Library for permission to reproduce the photographs used on pages 26, 49 and 55.

Data used to construct the UK population pyramid on page 34 © Crown copyright reproduced under the terms of the Click-Use Licence.

World Population Graph on page 39 reproduced with kind permission from Jean-Paul Rodrigue (underlying data from the United Nations).

Map of drought risk on page 62 © 'UCL Global Drought Monitor'.

Graph of the last 150 years of climate change on page 81 adapted from Crown Copyright data supplied by the Met Office.

Data used to compile the UK population density map on page 98 from Office for National Statistics: General Register Office for Scotland, Northern Ireland Statistics & Research Agency. © Crown copyright reproduced under the terms of the Click-Use Licence.

Data used to construct the flow map of immigration on page 102 © Crown copyright reproduced under the terms of the Click-Use Licence.

Printed by Elanders Ltd, Newcastle upon Tyne.
Clipart from Corel®

Based on the classic CGP style created by Richard Parsons.

Structure of the Course

'Know thy enemy', 'forewarned is forearmed'... There are many boring quotes that just mean <u>being prepared is a good thing</u>. <u>Don't</u> stumble <u>blindly</u> into a GCSE course — find out what you're facing.

You'll have to do Two Exams and a Report

GCSE Geography's divided into <u>three units</u> — <u>Unit B561: Sustainable Decision-Making Exercise (SDME)</u>, <u>Unit B562: Geographical Enquiry</u> and <u>Unit B563: Key Themes</u>. You'll have to do <u>two exams</u> — one for <u>Unit B561</u> and one for <u>Unit B563</u>. You'll also have to do a <u>report</u> for <u>Unit B562: Geographical Enquiry</u>.

Unit B563: Key Themes Exam

1) Unit B563's divided into <u>four Key Themes</u>:

- Theme 1 — Rivers and Coasts
- Theme 2 — Population and Settlement
- Theme 3 — Natural Hazards
- Theme 4 — Economic Development

1 hour 45 minutes

99 marks in total

50% of your final mark

2) The exam will cover <u>three of the four</u> themes <u>each year</u>.
3) Which three themes are covered will <u>change each year</u>, so <u>ask your teacher</u>.
4) The <u>fourth</u> Key Theme will be <u>tested</u> in the <u>SDME exam</u> (<u>Unit B561</u>).
5) You need to <u>answer all the questions</u> in this paper.

Unit B561: SDME Exam

1) The <u>SDME</u> is a <u>decision-making exam</u> based on <u>one of the Key Themes</u> — which one it's based on will <u>change each year</u>, so <u>ask your teacher</u>. E.g. one year it'll be <u>Rivers and Coasts</u>, and the <u>Key Theme exam</u> (<u>Unit B563</u>) will cover the <u>other three</u> themes.

2) In the exam you'll be given a <u>resource booklet</u>. You need to <u>study</u> it, then use the information (along with your <u>own knowledge</u>) to answer the <u>questions</u>.

3) You might also have to <u>answer some background questions</u> on the Key Theme — so you <u>need to revise all the information</u> for that theme.

4) The <u>final question</u> will ask you to <u>make a decision</u> (i.e. <u>decide what should be done</u>) — use your <u>background information</u> and the <u>resource booklet</u> to help you.

5) You need to <u>answer all the questions</u> in this paper.

1 hour 30 minutes

40 marks in total

25% of your final mark

Unit B562: Geographical Enquiry

The <u>Geographical Enquiry</u> involves some <u>fieldwork</u> (outdoor fun, often in wellies) and a <u>report</u> — it used to be called <u>coursework</u>.

Around 16 hours of class time

60 marks in total
25% of your final mark

Suggested word limit: 2000

1) The fieldwork involves collecting <u>primary data</u> (data you collect <u>yourself</u>, e.g. measurements of beach width).

2) In the <u>written report</u> you need to explain <u>what you found out</u> (see pages 90-95). It's done under <u>controlled conditions</u> (a bit like exam conditions).

This book only has one key theme — revision...

Exam boards like to give exams <u>confusing names</u> — they could have called them unit 1, 2 and 3... Anyhoo, now you know what's what you're totally prepped for the exam (yay). Well almost, there's just a bookful of stuff to <u>learn</u> first...

How to Use This Book

That last page was a bit scary, talking about <u>exams</u> when you haven't even started <u>revising</u> yet. But don't worry — this book's here to help when you do start revising, so you'll ace your exams.

This Book's in the Same Order as the Course

This book is arranged to follow the <u>structure of the course</u> (see previous page). It covers <u>all the Key Themes</u>, split into <u>smaller sections</u>, which makes them easier to digest:

- <u>Rivers and Coasts</u> — is covered by <u>Section 1</u> (<u>Rivers</u>) and <u>Section 2</u> (<u>Coasts</u>).
- <u>Population and Settlement</u> — is covered by <u>Section 3</u> (<u>Population</u>) and <u>Section 4</u> (<u>Settlement</u>).
- <u>Natural Hazards</u> — is covered by <u>Section 5</u> (<u>Tectonic Hazards</u>) and <u>Section 6</u> (<u>Climatic Hazards</u>).
- <u>Economic Development</u> — is covered by <u>Section 7</u> (<u>Development</u>), <u>Section 8</u> (<u>Industry</u>) and <u>Section 9</u> (<u>Globalisation</u>).

Work out which themes you're weakest on — you should spend longest revising these.

You Have to Study All the Key Themes

1) You will be <u>tested</u> on <u>all the Key Themes</u>, across <u>two exams</u>. So you need to <u>revise ALL the material</u> covered in this book.

2) The <u>SDME exam</u> (<u>Unit B561</u>) will cover <u>one Key Theme</u>, which <u>changes each year</u>. You could <u>circle the sections</u> that cover that Key Theme on the <u>contents page</u> of this book. Then you'll know to <u>revise those sections nearest</u> to your SDME exam.

3) The <u>Key Themes exam</u> (<u>Unit B563</u>) will cover the <u>other three themes</u> — you could <u>circle</u> these in a <u>different colour</u> so you <u>revise just these</u> before your Key Themes exam.

Don't scribble on your book if it's a school copy.

Add to this Book and Practise, Practise, Practise

This book covers <u>all you need to know</u>, but for <u>top marks</u>, there are a couple of <u>other things</u> you can do:

Make your own notes

<u>Add your own notes</u> or put pages of your class notes into this book, e.g. you might not like the <u>case studies</u> on the earthquakes in Italy and Pakistan — so <u>stick</u> your own case studies in that place instead (just make sure they <u>cover the same points</u>).

Case Study #4
Pros: Holds lots of paper.
Cons: Doesn't fasten.

Practise exam questions

1) This book contains <u>everything</u> you need to <u>revise</u>, but you need to do <u>practice exam questions too</u>.

2) There's a handy <u>Exam Skills</u> section that should help with all the different <u>skills</u> you might need in an exam, but you still need to actually <u>practise</u> them.

3) Try having a go at some <u>past exam papers</u> (ask your teacher where to find these).

Practise exams — as if life isn't bad enough already...

Well, now you know <u>what's coming your way</u> and <u>how to use this book</u>, the time has come when you've got to <u>sit down</u> and do the <u>revision</u>. Don't worry though, I'll be here every step of the way to keep you <u>entertained</u>.

The Hydrological Cycle

Since this is the first page of the book I'm going to be nice and treat you to <u>something special</u> — the <u>hydrological cycle</u> (a.k.a. the <u>water cycle</u> in non-geography lingo). Knock yourself out...

The Hydrological Cycle Shows How Water Moves Around

1) The hydrological cycle has <u>different parts</u> — the <u>sea</u>, the <u>land</u> and the <u>atmosphere</u>.

2) Water <u>flows</u> between the different parts in various ways, and is also <u>stored</u> on the <u>land</u> (see below).

3) The hydrological cycle is a <u>closed system</u>. This means there are <u>no inputs</u> (water going <u>in</u>) or <u>outputs</u> (water going <u>out</u>) — the water just <u>flows round and round</u> the cycle:

① Water <u>evaporates</u> from the <u>sea</u> and the <u>land</u> — <u>evaporation</u> is when water is <u>heated</u> by the <u>sun</u> and <u>turns into water vapour</u>. <u>Transpiration</u> is the <u>evaporation</u> of water from <u>plants</u>. <u>Evapotranspiration</u> is both <u>evaporation</u> and <u>transpiration happening together</u>.

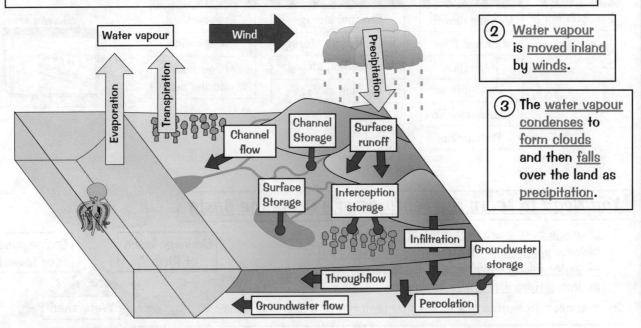

② <u>Water vapour</u> is <u>moved inland</u> by <u>winds</u>.

③ The <u>water vapour</u> <u>condenses</u> to <u>form clouds</u> and then <u>falls</u> over the land as <u>precipitation</u>.

④ Water <u>moves from one place to another</u> in many ways (called <u>flows</u> or <u>transfers</u>):
- <u>Infiltration</u> is when water <u>soaks into the soil</u>.
- <u>Percolation</u> is when water <u>moves vertically down</u> through <u>soil</u> and <u>rock</u>.
- <u>Throughflow</u> is when water in the <u>soil</u> flows downhill.
- <u>Groundwater flow</u> is when water in <u>rock</u> flows downhill.
- <u>Surface runoff</u> is when <u>water flows overground</u>.
- <u>Channel flow</u> is the <u>flow of water in a river</u>.

The movement of water vapour by wind is also a flow.

⑤ Water can also be <u>held</u> on the land in <u>stores</u>:
- <u>Channel storage</u> is when water is <u>held in a river</u>.
- <u>Groundwater storage</u> is when water is stored underground in soil and rock. A <u>rock</u> that <u>stores water</u> is called an <u>aquifer</u>, e.g. chalk.
- <u>Interception storage</u> is when water <u>lands</u> on things like <u>plant leaves</u> and <u>doesn't hit the ground</u>.
- <u>Surface storage</u> is when water is held in things like <u>lakes</u>, <u>reservoirs</u> and <u>puddles</u>.

⑥ The water eventually <u>ends up in the sea</u>, where it <u>evaporates</u> and <u>goes round the cycle again</u>...

Percolation and infiltration — sounds like a recipe for a great cuppa...

Crikey, there are a lot of <u>geography terms</u> to get your head round on this page — make sure you understand what <u>each one means</u>. To check, shut the book and scribble out as many as you can remember (no sneaky peeking either).

Drainage Basins

If you've had a crack at the <u>hydrological cycle</u> then <u>drainage basins</u> should be a doddle — they're just a <u>part</u> of the hydrological cycle. But you'll need to know a little bit more than that, so have a read...

A Drainage Basin is the Area of Land Drained by a River

1) The part of the <u>hydrological cycle</u> that happens <u>on land</u> goes on in <u>drainage basins</u>.

2) Drainage basins are <u>open systems</u>:
   - There are <u>inputs</u> of water to drainage basins.
   - Water <u>flows through them</u> and is <u>stored in them</u>.
   - There are <u>outputs</u> of water from drainage basins.

Here's a handy table to show you <u>what's going on</u>:

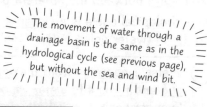

The movement of water through a drainage basin is the same as in the hydrological cycle (see previous page), but without the sea and wind bit.

INPUTS	FLOWS	STORES	OUTPUTS
Precipitation	Surface runoff	Channel storage	Evaporation
	Channel flow	Groundwater storage	Transpiration
	Infiltration	Interception storage	River flow into the sea
	Throughflow	Surface storage	
	Groundwater flow		
	Percolation		

You Need to Learn the Features of a Drainage Basin

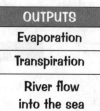

1) <u>Drainage basins</u> are <u>separated</u> by a <u>boundary</u> called a <u>watershed</u>. They're <u>ridges of high land</u> — <u>water falling either side</u> of these ridges will go into <u>different drainage basins</u>.

Drainage basin of River A | Drainage basin of River B | Watershed

2) You need to learn a <u>few</u> of the <u>key features</u> of a drainage basin:
   - A <u>tributary</u> is a <u>smaller river</u> (e.g. a stream) that <u>joins</u> a <u>main river</u>.
   - The <u>source</u> is where a river <u>starts</u>, usually in an <u>upland area</u> (e.g. mountains).
   - A <u>confluence</u> is a <u>point</u> where <u>two rivers join</u>.
   - The <u>mouth</u> is where a river <u>flows into the sea</u> or a <u>lake</u>.

Some drainage basins are massive, e.g. the drainage basin of the Amazon River is more than 6 million km².

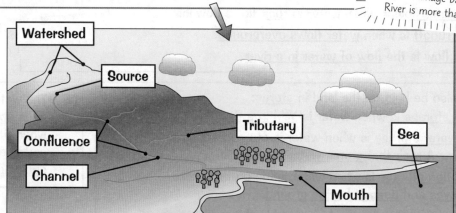

Drainage basin — not a fancy word for a colander...

I thought a tributary was someone who covers old pop songs in a dodgy pub, but you learn something new every day. Speaking of learning, make sure you can name all the <u>inputs</u>, <u>flows</u>, <u>stores</u> and <u>outputs</u> of a <u>drainage basin system</u>.

Weathering and the River Valley

You won't find much chocolate in a <u>drainage basin</u>, but you will find <u>rocks</u>, <u>river valleys</u> and ramblers...

Rocks in a Drainage Basin are Broken Down by Weathering

Weathering happens in drainage basins — it's the <u>breakdown</u> of rocks <u>where they are</u> (the material created doesn't get taken away like with erosion). There are three main types of weathering:

1) <u>Mechanical weathering</u> is the <u>breakdown</u> of rock <u>without changing</u> its <u>chemical composition</u>. <u>Freeze-thaw weathering</u> is a type of mechanical weathering that happens in drainage basins:

   1) It happens when the temperature <u>alternates above</u> and <u>below 0 °C</u> (the <u>freezing point</u> of water).
   2) Water <u>gets into</u> rock that has <u>cracks</u>, e.g. granite.
   3) When the water <u>freezes</u> it <u>expands</u>, which puts <u>pressure</u> on the rock.
   4) When the water <u>thaws</u> it <u>contracts</u>, which <u>releases</u> the <u>pressure</u> on the rock.
   5) <u>Repeated freezing</u> and <u>thawing</u> widens the cracks and causes the rock to <u>break up</u>.

2) <u>Chemical weathering</u> is the breakdown of rock by <u>changing</u> its <u>chemical composition</u>. <u>Carbonation weathering</u> is a type of chemical weathering that happens in <u>warm</u> and <u>wet</u> conditions:

   1) Rainwater has <u>carbon dioxide</u> dissolved in it, which makes it a <u>weak carbonic acid</u>.
   2) Carbonic acid <u>reacts</u> with rock that contains <u>calcium carbonate</u>, e.g. limestone, so the <u>rocks</u> are <u>dissolved</u> by the rainwater.

3) <u>Biological weathering</u> is the breakdown of rocks by <u>living things</u>, e.g. <u>plant roots</u> break down rocks by <u>growing into cracks</u> on their surfaces and <u>pushing them apart</u>.

A River's Long Profile and Cross Profile Vary Over its Course

1) The <u>path</u> of a river as it <u>flows downhill</u> is called its <u>course</u>.
2) Rivers have an <u>upper course</u> (closest to the <u>source</u> of the river), a <u>middle course</u> and a <u>lower course</u> (closest to the <u>mouth</u> of the river).
3) Rivers flow in <u>channels</u> in <u>valleys</u>.
4) They <u>erode</u> the landscape — <u>wear it down</u>, then <u>transport</u> the material to somewhere else where it's <u>deposited</u>.
5) The <u>shape</u> of the <u>valley</u> and <u>channel changes</u> along the river depending on whether <u>erosion</u> or <u>deposition</u> is having the <u>most impact</u> (is the <u>dominant process</u>).
6) The <u>long profile</u> of a river shows you how the <u>gradient</u> (steepness) <u>changes</u> over the different courses.
7) The <u>cross profile</u> shows you what a <u>cross-section</u> of the river looks like.

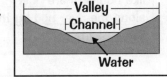

Course	Gradient	Valley and channel shape	Cross profile
Upper	Steep	<u>V-shaped</u> valley, steep sides. <u>Narrow</u>, <u>shallow</u> channel.	
Middle	Medium	<u>Gently sloping</u> valley sides. <u>Wider</u>, <u>deeper</u> channel.	
Lower	Gentle	<u>Very wide</u>, almost flat valley. <u>Very wide</u>, <u>deep</u> channel.	

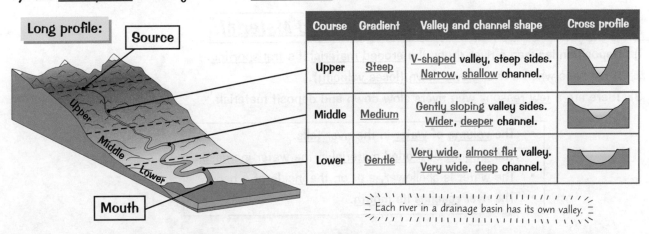

Long profile: Source — Upper — Middle — Lower — Mouth

Each river in a drainage basin has its own valley.

The river valet was rubbish at his job — all the cars got soaked...

There seems like a lot on this page but it's all pretty <u>straightforward</u>. You need to know <u>river profiles</u> like the back of your hand — try <u>drawing</u> the <u>cross profile diagrams</u> and <u>describing</u> the <u>shape</u> of the <u>valley</u> and <u>channel</u>.

Erosion, Transportation and Deposition

Rivers <u>scrape</u> and <u>smash rocks up</u>, <u>push</u> them about, then <u>dump them</u> when they've had enough...

There are Four Processes of Erosion

1) <u>Hydraulic action</u>

> The <u>force</u> of the water <u>breaks rock particles away</u> from the <u>river channel</u>.

2) <u>Corrasion</u>

> Eroded <u>rocks</u> picked up by the river <u>scrape</u> and <u>rub</u> against the <u>channel</u>, wearing it away. <u>Most erosion</u> happens by <u>corrasion</u>.

3) <u>Attrition</u>

> Eroded <u>rocks</u> picked up by the river <u>smash into each other</u> and break into <u>smaller fragments</u>. Their <u>edges</u> also get <u>rounded off</u> as they rub together.

4) <u>Corrosion</u>

> River water <u>dissolves</u> some types of rock, e.g. <u>chalk</u> and <u>limestone</u>.

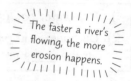

I'm taking hydraulic action against this revision.

The faster a river's flowing, the more erosion happens.

Transportation <u>is</u> the Movement <u>of</u> Eroded Material

The <u>material</u> a river has <u>eroded</u> is <u>transported downstream</u>.
There are <u>four processes</u> of transportation:

1. <u>Traction</u> — <u>large</u> particles like boulders are <u>pushed</u> along the <u>river bed</u> by the <u>force of the water</u>.

2. <u>Saltation</u> — <u>pebble-sized</u> particles are <u>bounced along</u> the <u>river bed</u> by the <u>force of the water</u>.

3. <u>Suspension</u> — <u>small</u> particles like silt and clay are <u>carried along</u> by the water.

4. <u>Solution</u> — <u>soluble materials</u> <u>dissolve</u> in the water and are <u>carried along</u>.

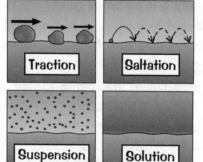

Traction   Saltation   Suspension   Solution

Deposition <u>is</u> When a River Drops Eroded Material

1) Deposition is when a river <u>drops</u> the <u>eroded material</u> it's <u>transporting</u>.

2) It happens when a river <u>slows down</u> (<u>loses velocity</u>).

3) There are a <u>few reasons</u> why rivers slow down and deposit material:

> - The <u>volume</u> of <u>water</u> in the river <u>falls</u>.
> - The <u>amount</u> of <u>eroded material</u> in the water <u>increases</u>.
> - The water is <u>shallower</u>, e.g. on the <u>inside of a bend</u>.
> - The river <u>reaches</u> its <u>mouth</u>.

In rock school there's only one punishment for naughty gravel — suspension...

There are loads of amazingly similar names to remember here — try not to confuse <u>saltation</u>, <u>solution</u> and <u>suspension</u>, and don't mix up <u>corrasion</u> and <u>corrosion</u>. Otherwise you'll regret it. Now saltate on over to the next page...

Erosional River Landforms

If you don't know anything about <u>waterfalls</u> then you haven't been watching enough <u>shampoo adverts</u>. Now's your chance to find out all about them and other landforms made by erosion.

Waterfalls and Gorges are Found in the Upper Course of a River

1) <u>Waterfalls</u> (e.g. High Force waterfall on the River Tees) form where a river flows over an area of <u>hard rock</u> followed by an area of <u>softer rock</u>.

2) The <u>softer rock</u> is <u>eroded more</u> than the <u>hard rock</u>, creating a '<u>step</u>' in the river.

3) As water goes over the step it <u>erodes more and more</u> of the softer rock.

4) A <u>steep drop</u> is eventually created, which is called a <u>waterfall</u>.

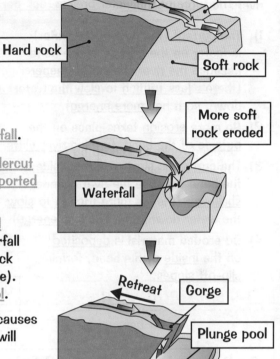

5) The <u>hard rock</u> is eventually <u>undercut</u> by erosion. It becomes <u>unsupported</u> and <u>collapses</u>.

6) The collapsed rocks are <u>swirled around</u> at the foot of the waterfall where they <u>erode</u> the softer rock by <u>corrasion</u> (see previous page). This creates a deep <u>plunge pool</u>.

7) Over time, <u>more undercutting</u> causes <u>more collapses</u>. The waterfall will <u>retreat</u> (move back up the channel), leaving behind a steep-sided <u>gorge</u>.

Interlocking Spurs are Nothing to do with Cowboys

1) In the <u>upper course</u> of a river most of the <u>erosion</u> is <u>vertically downwards</u>. This creates <u>steep-sided</u>, <u>V-shaped valleys</u>.

2) The rivers <u>aren't powerful enough</u> to <u>erode laterally</u> (sideways) — they have to <u>wind around</u> the <u>high hillsides</u> that stick out into their paths on either side.

3) The <u>hillsides that interlock</u> with each other (like a zip if you were looking from above) as the river winds around them are called <u>interlocking spurs</u>.

Interlocking spurs along a river in Georgia

Some river landforms are beautiful — others are gorge-ous...

Step over the <u>hard rock</u> and <u>plunge</u> into the <u>pool</u> — that's how I remember how <u>waterfalls</u> are formed. Geography examiners <u>love river landforms</u> (they're a bit weird like that) so make sure you learn <u>how they form</u>.

Erosional and Depositional River Landforms

When a river's <u>eroding</u> and <u>depositing</u> material, <u>meanders</u> and <u>ox-bow lakes</u> can form. Australians have a different name for <u>ox-bow lakes</u> — billabongs. Stay tuned for more incredible facts.

Meanders are Large Bends in a River

In their <u>middle</u> and <u>lower courses</u>, rivers develop <u>meanders</u>:

1) The <u>current</u> (the flow of the water) is <u>faster</u> on the <u>outside</u> of the bend because the river channel is <u>deeper</u> (there's <u>less friction</u> to <u>slow</u> the water down, so it has <u>more energy</u>).

2) So more <u>erosion</u> takes place on the <u>outside</u> of the bend, forming <u>river cliffs</u>.

3) The <u>current</u> is <u>slower</u> on the <u>inside</u> of the bend because the river channel is <u>shallower</u> (there's <u>more friction</u> to <u>slow</u> the water down, so it has <u>less energy</u>).

4) So eroded material is <u>deposited</u> on the <u>inside</u> of the bend, forming <u>slip-off slopes</u>.

The Mississippi River in the USA has lots of meanders.

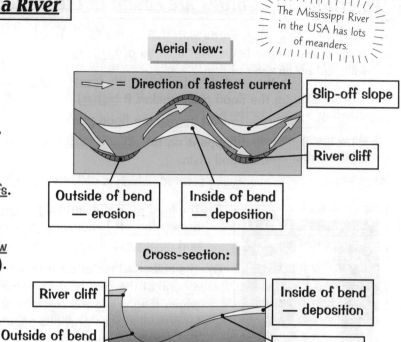

Aerial view:

= Direction of fastest current

Slip-off slope

River cliff

Outside of bend — erosion

Inside of bend — deposition

Cross-section:

River cliff

Inside of bend — deposition

Outside of bend — erosion

Slip-off slope

Ox-Bow Lakes are Formed from Meanders

Meanders get <u>larger</u> over time — they can eventually turn into an <u>ox-bow lake</u>:

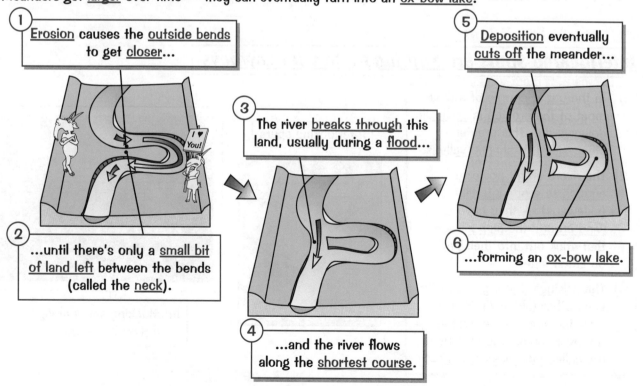

1 <u>Erosion</u> causes the <u>outside bends</u> to get <u>closer</u>...

2 ...until there's only a <u>small bit of land left</u> between the bends (called the <u>neck</u>).

3 The river <u>breaks through</u> this land, usually during a <u>flood</u>...

4 ...and the river flows along the <u>shortest course</u>.

5 <u>Deposition</u> eventually <u>cuts off</u> the meander...

6 ...forming an <u>ox-bow lake</u>.

Ox-bow lakes — where ox-tail soup comes from...

In the exam, don't be afraid to draw <u>diagrams</u> of <u>river landforms</u> — examiners love a good diagram. Don't worry about it being a pretty picture though, it's just there to make your answer clearer. This time, meander over to the next page...

Depositional River Landforms

When <u>rivers dump material</u> they don't do it by text message — they make attractive <u>landforms</u> instead.

Flood Plains <u>are</u> Flat Areas of Land that Flood

1) The <u>flood plain</u> is the <u>wide valley floor</u> on either side of a river which occasionally <u>gets flooded</u>.

2) When a river <u>floods</u> onto the flood plain, the water <u>slows down</u> and <u>deposits</u> the <u>eroded material</u> that it's <u>transporting</u>. This <u>builds up</u> the flood plain (makes it <u>higher</u>).

3) <u>Meanders migrate</u> (move) <u>across</u> the flood plain, making it <u>wider</u>.

4) The <u>deposition</u> that happens on the <u>slip-off slopes</u> of meanders also <u>builds up</u> the flood plain.

Flood plain

All these landforms are found in the lower course of a river.

Levees <u>are</u> Natural Embankments

Levees are <u>natural embankments</u> (raised bits) along the <u>edges</u> of a <u>river channel</u>. During a flood, <u>eroded material</u> is <u>deposited</u> over the whole flood plain. The <u>heaviest material</u> is <u>deposited closest</u> to the river channel, because it gets <u>dropped first</u> when the river <u>slows down</u>. <u>Over time</u>, the <u>deposited material builds up</u>, creating <u>levees</u> along the edges of the channel, e.g. along the Yellow River in China.

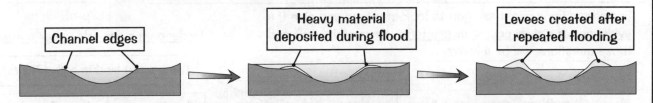

Channel edges

Heavy material deposited during flood

Levees created after repeated flooding

Deltas <u>are</u> Low-Lying Areas <u>Where a River Meets the Sea or a Lake</u>

1) Rivers are <u>forced to slow down</u> when they <u>meet the sea</u> or a <u>lake</u>. This causes them to <u>deposit</u> the <u>material</u> that they're carrying.

2) If the <u>sea doesn't wash away</u> the <u>material</u> it <u>builds up</u> and the <u>channel gets blocked</u>. This forces the channel to <u>split up</u> into <u>lots of smaller rivers</u> called <u>distributaries</u>.

3) Eventually the <u>material builds up so much</u> that <u>low-lying areas of land</u> called <u>deltas</u> are <u>formed</u>.

4) There are <u>three types</u> of delta:

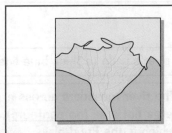

<u>Arcuate</u> — have a <u>rounded shape</u> and <u>lots of distributaries</u>, e.g. the Nile delta.

<u>Cuspate</u> — have a <u>triangular shape</u> and <u>few distributaries</u>, e.g. the Tiber delta.

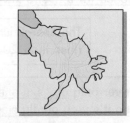

<u>Bird's foot</u> — wait for it... are <u>shaped like a bird's foot</u>, e.g. the Mississippi delta.

<u>Yeah, it looks like a bird's foot — if the bird landed in a blender...</u>

I'll be the first person to admit that these <u>depositional landforms</u> aren't as exciting as waterfalls, but you still need to know about them. The only <u>tricky bits</u> on this page are the <u>names</u> of the <u>types of delta</u> — the <u>rest</u> is a <u>piece of cake</u>.

Rivers on Maps

You can know all the facts about <u>rivers</u>, but if you don't know what their <u>features</u> look like on <u>maps</u> then some of the exam questions will be a wee bit tricky. Here's something I prepared earlier...

Contour Lines Tell you the Direction a River Flows

<u>Contour lines</u> are the <u>orange lines</u> drawn all over maps. They tell you about the <u>height</u> of the land (in metres) by the numbers marked on them, and the <u>steepness</u> of the land by how <u>close together</u> they are (the <u>closer</u> they are, the <u>steeper</u> the slope).

It sounds obvious, but rivers <u>can't</u> flow uphill. Unless gravity's gone screwy, a river flows <u>from higher</u> contour lines <u>to lower</u> ones. Have a look at this map of Cawfell Beck:

Take a peek at pages 103-104 for more on reading maps.

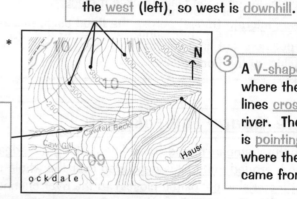

① The <u>height values</u> get <u>smaller</u> towards the <u>west</u> (left), so west is <u>downhill</u>.

② Cawfell Beck is flowing from <u>east</u> to <u>west</u> (right to left).

③ A <u>V-shape</u> is formed where the contour lines <u>cross</u> the river. The V-shape is <u>pointing uphill</u> to where the river came from.

Maps contain Evidence for River Courses and Landforms

Exam questions might ask you to look at a <u>map</u> and give the <u>evidence</u> for a <u>river course</u> or <u>landform</u>. Learn this stuff and those questions will be a breeze:

Evidence for a river's upper course

The nearby land is <u>high</u> (712 m).

The river <u>crosses lots</u> of <u>contour lines</u> in a <u>short distance</u>, which means it's <u>steep</u>.

The river's <u>narrow</u> (a <u>thin</u> blue line).

The <u>contour lines</u> are very <u>close together</u> and the valley floor is narrow. This means the river is in a <u>steep-sided V-shaped</u> valley.

Evidence for a waterfall

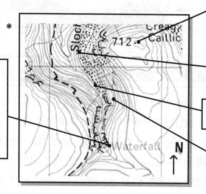

<u>Waterfalls</u> are marked on maps, but the <u>symbol for a cliff</u> (black, blocky lines) and the <u>close contour lines</u> are evidence for a waterfall.

Evidence for a river's lower course

The nearby land is <u>low</u> (less than 20 m).

The river only <u>crosses one contour line</u> so it's <u>very gently sloping</u>.

Another piece of evidence would be the river <u>joining</u> a <u>sea</u> or <u>lake</u>.

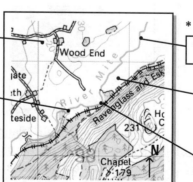

The river's <u>wide</u> (a <u>thick</u> blue line).

The river meanders across a large flat area (<u>no contours</u>), which is the <u>flood plain</u>.

The river has <u>large meanders</u>.

A cup of hot chocolate, a roaring fire and a good map — my idea of a fun night in...

<u>Map</u> questions can be a gold mine of easy marks — all you have to do is <u>say what you see</u>. You just need to understand what the maps are <u>showing</u>, so read this page like there's no tomorrow, then see if you can remember it all.

River Valley — Case Study

I know what you're thinking — we're over 10 pages into this geography book and there's not been a <u>case study</u> yet. Well, thank your lucky stars because I've got a real treat lined up for you — we're off to Glasgow...

The River Clyde Flows Through Scotland

1) The River Clyde is about <u>160 km long</u>.

2) Its <u>source</u> is in the <u>Southern Uplands region</u> of <u>Scotland</u> and the river <u>flows north-west</u> through <u>Motherwell</u> and <u>Glasgow</u>.

3) The <u>mouth</u> of the River Clyde is an <u>estuary</u> on the <u>west coast</u> of Scotland.

4) Here are some of the <u>features</u> and <u>landforms</u> in the <u>valley</u> that the <u>River Clyde</u> flows through:

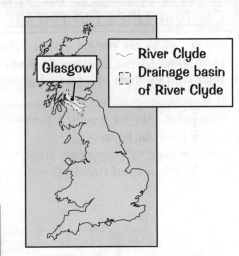

Glasgow

~ River Clyde
□ Drainage basin of River Clyde

\\\|||||||||||||||||///
An estuary is the mouth
of a river that joins the sea.
///||||||||||||||\\\

The River Clyde's flood plain
©iStockphoto.com/Martin McCarthy

The river's <u>estuary</u> is about <u>34 km west</u> of <u>Glasgow</u> — the <u>estuary</u> is about <u>3 km wide</u>. The <u>river joins</u> the <u>Firth of Clyde</u>, which eventually becomes the <u>Irish Sea</u>.

<u>Glasgow</u> is <u>built on</u> the <u>flood plain</u> of the River Clyde. The land is about <u>5 m above sea level</u> on <u>either side of the river</u>.

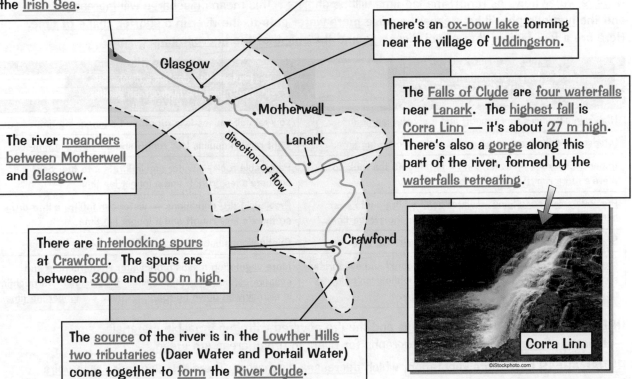

Glasgow

• Motherwell

Lanark

direction of flow

• Crawford

There's an <u>ox-bow lake</u> forming near the village of <u>Uddingston</u>.

The <u>Falls of Clyde</u> are <u>four waterfalls</u> near <u>Lanark</u>. The <u>highest fall</u> is <u>Corra Linn</u> — it's about <u>27 m high</u>. There's also a <u>gorge</u> along this part of the river, formed by the <u>waterfalls retreating</u>.

The river <u>meanders</u> <u>between Motherwell</u> and <u>Glasgow</u>.

There are <u>interlocking spurs</u> at <u>Crawford</u>. The spurs are between <u>300</u> and <u>500 m high</u>.

The <u>source</u> of the river is in the <u>Lowther Hills</u> — <u>two tributaries</u> (Daer Water and Portail Water) come together to <u>form</u> the <u>River Clyde</u>.

Corra Linn
©iStockphoto.com

Jocky and Clyde — doesn't really have the same ring to it...

What a lovely <u>case study</u> to ease you in with. You don't have to thank me, but it would be nice. Anyway, make sure you know the <u>River Clyde's</u> vital statistics — <u>landforms</u>, <u>place names</u> and <u>measurements</u>. Job done. Let's move on...

The Storm Hydrograph

We've not really talked much about the actual <u>water</u> in a river. Well, all that's about to change — hooray.

River Discharge is the Volume of Water Flowing in a River

River discharge is simply the <u>volume of water</u> that flows in a river <u>per second</u>. It's measured in <u>cumecs</u> — cubic metres per second (m^3/s). <u>Hydrographs</u> show how the discharge at a <u>certain point</u> in a river <u>changes</u> over time. <u>Storm hydrographs</u> show the changes in river discharge around the time of a <u>storm</u>. Here's an example of a storm hydrograph:

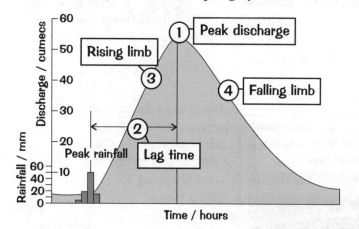

① <u>Peak discharge</u>:
The <u>highest discharge</u> in the period of time you're looking at.

② <u>Lag time</u>:
The <u>delay</u> between <u>peak rainfall</u> and <u>peak discharge</u>.

③ <u>Rising limb</u>:
The <u>increase</u> in river discharge as <u>rainwater</u> flows into the river.

④ <u>Falling limb</u>:
The <u>decrease</u> in river discharge as the river returns to its <u>normal level</u>.

Lag time happens because most rainwater <u>doesn't land directly</u> in the river channel — there's a <u>delay</u> as rainwater <u>gets to the channel</u>. It gets there by <u>flowing quickly overland</u> (called <u>surface runoff</u>, or just <u>runoff</u>), or by <u>soaking into the ground</u> (called <u>infiltration</u>) and flowing <u>slowly underground</u>.

River Discharge is Affected by Different Factors

If <u>more water</u> flows as <u>runoff</u> the <u>lag time</u> will be <u>shorter</u>. This means <u>discharge</u> will <u>increase</u> and the <u>hydrograph</u> will be <u>steeper</u> because <u>more water</u> gets to the river in a <u>shorter space of time</u>. Here are a few <u>factors</u> that affect <u>discharge</u> and the <u>shape</u> of the <u>hydrograph</u>:

Factors that increase discharge and make the hydrograph steeper	Factors that decrease discharge and make the hydrograph gentler
<u>High rainfall</u> causes <u>more runoff</u> and a <u>shorter lag time</u>.	<u>Low rainfall</u> causes <u>less runoff</u> and a <u>longer lag time</u>.
<u>Intense rainfall</u> causes <u>more runoff</u> and a <u>shorter lag time</u>.	<u>Light rainfall</u> causes <u>less runoff</u> and a <u>longer lag time</u>.
<u>Impermeable rock</u> — water <u>can't infiltrate</u> into the rock so there's <u>more runoff</u> and a <u>shorter lag time</u>.	<u>Permeable rock</u> — water <u>can infiltrate</u> into the rock so there's <u>less runoff</u> and a <u>longer lag time</u>.
<u>Previously wet conditions</u> — water <u>can't infiltrate</u> into <u>saturated soil</u> so there's <u>more runoff</u> and a <u>shorter lag time</u>.	<u>Previously dry conditions</u> — water <u>can infiltrate</u> into <u>dry soil</u> so there's <u>less runoff</u> and a <u>longer lag time</u>.
<u>Steep slopes</u> cause <u>more runoff</u> and a <u>shorter lag time</u>.	<u>Gentle slopes</u> cause <u>less runoff</u> and a <u>longer lag time</u>.
<u>Less vegetation</u> means <u>less water is intercepted</u> and evaporates so <u>more water reaches the channel</u>. <u>Throughflow isn't slowed down by roots</u>, so there's a <u>shorter lag time</u>.	<u>More vegetation</u> means <u>more water is intercepted</u> and <u>evaporates</u>, so <u>less water reaches the channel</u>. <u>Throughflow</u> is also <u>slowed down by roots</u>, so there's a <u>longer lag time</u>.

<u>URBAN AREAS</u> have <u>drainage systems</u> and they're covered with <u>impermeable materials</u> — these <u>increase discharge</u> so hydrographs for rivers in urban areas are <u>steep</u>.

<u>RURAL AREAS</u> have <u>more vegetation</u>, which <u>decreases discharge</u>. There are also <u>more reservoirs</u> in rural areas — they <u>store water</u> and <u>release it slowly</u>, <u>decreasing discharge</u> in the river below. This means hydrographs for rivers in rural areas are more <u>gently sloping</u>.

Revision lag time — the time between starting and getting bored...

You need to know how <u>different factors</u> can affect the <u>discharge</u> of a river and <u>hydrographs</u> are a helpful way of understanding what's going on. They sound like something from the future, but the excitement ends there I'm afraid.

Flooding — Causes

Flooding happens when the <u>level</u> of a river gets <u>so high</u> that it <u>spills over its banks</u> onto the <u>flood plain</u>. Floods can be caused by <u>Mother Nature</u>, or guess who else... you got it — us pesky <u>human beings</u>.

Rivers Flood due to Physical Factors

The <u>river level increases</u> when the <u>discharge increases</u> because a high discharge means there's <u>more water in the channel</u>. This means the factors that <u>increase discharge</u> can also <u>cause flooding</u>:

Prolonged rainfall

After a <u>long period</u> of rain, the soil becomes <u>saturated</u>. Any further rainfall <u>can't infiltrate</u>, which <u>increases runoff</u> into rivers. This <u>increases discharge quickly</u>, which can cause a flood.

Heavy rainfall

Heavy rainfall means there's <u>a lot of runoff</u>. This <u>increases discharge quickly</u>, which can cause a flood.

Snowmelt

When a lot of <u>snow</u> or <u>ice melts</u> it means that a <u>lot of water</u> goes into a river in a <u>short space of time</u>. This <u>increases discharge quickly</u>, which can cause a flood.

Relief (how the height of the land changes)

If a river is in a <u>steep-sided valley</u>, water will reach the river channel <u>much faster</u> because water <u>flows more quickly</u> on <u>steeper slopes</u>. This <u>increases discharge quickly</u>, which can cause a flood.

Geology

When a river is in an area of <u>permeable rock</u> (e.g. limestone), more water <u>percolates into the rock</u> instead of <u>flowing on the surface</u>. This means there's <u>less runoff</u>, so the risk of flooding is <u>lower</u>. When a river is in an area of <u>impermeable rock</u> (e.g. clay), water <u>doesn't percolate into the rock</u> but flows on the surface. This means there's <u>more runoff</u>, so the risk of flooding is <u>higher</u>.

Rivers also Flood because of Human Causes

Here are some examples of how <u>human actions</u> can make flooding <u>more frequent</u> and <u>more severe</u>:

Deforestation

Trees <u>intercept</u> (catch) rainwater on their leaves, which then <u>evaporates</u>. Trees also <u>take up water</u> from the ground and <u>store it</u>. This means <u>cutting down</u> trees <u>increases</u> the <u>volume</u> of water that <u>reaches</u> the river channel, which <u>increases discharge</u> and makes flooding <u>more likely</u>. Deforestation also causes <u>soil erosion</u> — there are no trees to <u>hold</u> the <u>soil together</u>, so it gets <u>washed away</u>. The soil ends up in the river, which <u>raises the riverbed</u>. This <u>reduces</u> the <u>volume of water</u> the river channel can hold, so the <u>risk of flooding is increased</u>.

Urbanisation

Urban areas have lots of <u>buildings</u> made from <u>impermeable materials</u> like concrete, and they're surrounded by <u>roads</u> made from <u>tarmac</u> (also impermeable). Impermeable surfaces <u>increase runoff</u> and <u>drains</u> quickly take runoff to rivers. This <u>increases discharge quickly</u>, which can cause a flood.

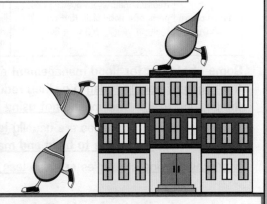

Eeek — everyone into the Ark...

There are plenty of things that can <u>cause a flood</u>, including a few that you probably wouldn't think of immediately. So, if your dad wants to tarmac the drive, then you can share your geography knowledge to warn him of the <u>risks</u>.

Flood Management

Floods can be <u>devastating</u>, but there are a number of different <u>strategies</u> to <u>stop them</u> or <u>lessen the blow</u>.

Floods have Some Serious Impacts

1) People are <u>killed</u> by <u>flood waters</u> or by the <u>other effects</u> of flooding, e.g. by the spread of <u>disease</u> when <u>water supplies</u> have been <u>contaminated</u> by <u>sewage</u> from <u>broken sewage pipes</u>.

2) <u>Buildings</u> are <u>damaged</u> or <u>destroyed</u>, making people <u>homeless</u> and causing <u>businesses to shut down</u>.

3) <u>Jobs are lost</u> because of damage to <u>premises</u> and <u>equipment</u>, or <u>pollution of farmland</u>.

The <u>effects</u> of flooding are <u>worse in LEDCs than MEDCs</u> because there's <u>less money</u> to spend on <u>flood protection</u> and to <u>help people</u> <u>after</u> a flood. Also, more people <u>live and work</u> in areas that are <u>likely to flood</u> and <u>poorer transport links</u> mean it's <u>more difficult</u> to <u>get help to places</u> that have been affected.

LEDCs are Less Economically Developed Countries (poor countries). MEDCs are More Economically Developed Countries (richer ones).

Hard and Soft Engineering can Reduce the Risk of Flooding or its Effects

<u>Hard engineering</u> — <u>man-made</u> <u>structures</u> built to <u>control the flow</u> of rivers and <u>reduce flooding</u>.

<u>Soft engineering</u> — schemes set up using <u>knowledge</u> of a <u>river</u> and its <u>processes</u> to <u>reduce the effects of flooding</u>.

Strategy	What it is	Benefits	Disadvantages
Dams and reservoirs	<u>Dams</u> (huge walls) are built <u>across</u> the rivers, usually in the <u>upper course</u>. A <u>reservoir</u> (artificial lake) is formed <u>behind</u> the dam.	Reservoirs <u>store water and release it slowly</u>, which <u>reduces</u> the <u>risk of flooding</u>. The water in the reservoir is used as <u>drinking water</u> and can be used to <u>generate hydroelectric power</u> (HEP). Reservoirs are also <u>attractive</u> and can be used for <u>recreation</u>.	Dams are <u>very expensive</u> to build. Creating a reservoir can <u>flood existing settlements</u>. Eroded material is <u>deposited</u> in the <u>reservoir</u> and <u>not</u> along the river's <u>natural course</u> making <u>farmland</u> downstream <u>less fertile</u>.
Channel straightening	The river's <u>course</u> is <u>straightened</u> — <u>meanders</u> are <u>cut out</u> by building <u>artificial straight channels</u>.	Water moves out of the area <u>more quickly</u> because it doesn't travel as far — <u>reducing</u> the <u>risk</u> of flooding.	<u>Flooding</u> may happen <u>downstream</u> of the straightened channel instead, as flood water is <u>carried there faster</u>.
Man-made levees	<u>Man-made embankments</u> along both sides of a river.	The embankments mean that the <u>river channel</u> can <u>hold more water</u>, which <u>reduces</u> the <u>risk of flooding</u>. They're also <u>quite cheap</u>.	If the levees <u>fail</u> (break) it can cause <u>catastrophic flooding</u>.
Flood warnings	People are <u>warned</u> about possible flooding through <u>TV</u>, <u>radio</u>, <u>newspapers</u> and <u>the internet</u>.	The <u>impact</u> of flooding is <u>reduced</u> — warnings give people time to <u>move possessions upstairs</u>, put <u>sandbags</u> in position and to <u>evacuate</u>.	Warnings <u>don't stop</u> a <u>flood</u> from happening. People may <u>not</u> hear or have <u>access</u> to warnings (especially in <u>LEDCs</u> where <u>communications</u> are <u>less developed</u>).
Preparation	Buildings are <u>modified</u> to <u>reduce</u> the amount of <u>damage</u> a flood could cause. People make <u>plans</u> for what to do in a flood, e.g. keep a blanket and torch in a handy place.	The <u>impact</u> of flooding is <u>reduced</u> — <u>buildings</u> are <u>less damaged</u> and people <u>know what to do</u> when a flood happens.	Preparation <u>doesn't guarantee safety</u> from a flood and it could give people a <u>false sense of security</u>. It's <u>expensive</u> to modify homes and businesses.
Flood plain zoning	Restrictions <u>prevent building</u> on parts of a flood plain that are <u>likely to be affected</u> by a flood.	The <u>risk of flooding</u> is <u>reduced</u> — <u>impermeable surfaces aren't created</u>, e.g. roads. The <u>impact</u> of flooding is <u>reduced</u> — there aren't any houses or roads to damage.	The <u>expansion</u> of an <u>urban area</u> is <u>limited</u> if there aren't any other suitable building sites. It's no help in areas that have <u>already been built on</u>.

Some strategies for flood management are <u>more sustainable than others</u>. Sustainable strategies meet the <u>needs</u> of <u>people today</u> (i.e. they reduce flooding), <u>without stopping people in the future</u> getting the things they <u>need</u>. This means <u>not using up resources</u> (e.g. money) or <u>damaging the environment</u>.

Hard engineering strategies are usually <u>less sustainable</u> than soft engineering strategies because they generally <u>cost more to build and maintain</u>, and they <u>damage the environment more</u>.

<u>Hard engineering</u> strategies are also <u>less suitable for LEDCs</u> as they're usually <u>really expensive</u>.

No, river straightening isn't done with a gigantic pair of hot ceramic plates...

Flooding can be a nightmare, especially if you live in an <u>LEDC</u>. But, as luck would have it, there are plenty of <u>strategies</u> to <u>reduce the impacts</u>. What's less lucky is the fact that you've got to <u>learn them all</u>, sigh.

Flooding — Case Studies

Oooh, time for a case study — everyone's favourite part of geography. Put your learning hat on...

MEDCs and LEDCs are Affected Differently by Flooding

The effects of floods and the responses to them are different in different parts of the world.
A lot depends on how wealthy the part of the world is. Learn the following case studies —
you might have to compare two floods like these in your exam:

Flood in an MEDC:

Place: Carlisle, England
Date: 8th January, 2005
River: Eden

Flood in an LEDC:

Place: South Asia (Bangladesh and India)
Date: July and August, 2007
Rivers: Brahmaputra and Ganges

	Carlisle, England	South Asia (Bangladesh and India)
Causes	• Heavy rainfall — 200 mm of rain fell in 36 hours. The continuous rainfall saturated the soil, increasing runoff into the River Eden. • Carlisle is a large urban area — impermeable materials like concrete increased runoff. • This caused the discharge of the River Eden to reach 1520 cumecs (its average discharge is 52 cumecs).	• Heavy rainfall — in one region, 900 mm of rain fell in July. The continuous rainfall saturated the soil, increasing runoff into rivers. • Melting snow from glaciers in the Himalayan mountains increased the discharge of the Brahmaputra river. • The peak discharge of both rivers happened at the same time, which increased discharge downstream.
Primary effects	• 3 deaths. • 4 schools were severely flooded. • 350 businesses were shut down. • 70 000 addresses lost power. • Some roads and bridges were damaged. • Rivers were polluted with rubbish and sewage.	• Over 2000 deaths. • 44 schools were totally destroyed. • Many factories closed and lots of livestock were killed. • 112 000 houses were destroyed in India. • 10 000 km of roads were destroyed. • Rivers were polluted with rubbish and sewage.
Secondary effects	• Around 3000 people were made homeless. • Children lost out on education — one school was closed for months. • Stress-related illnesses increased after the floods. • Around 3000 jobs were at risk in businesses affected by floods.	• Around 25 million people were made homeless. • Children lost out on education — around 4000 schools were affected by the floods. • Around 100 000 people caught water-borne diseases like dysentery and diarrhoea. • Flooded fields reduced basmati rice yields — prices rose 10%. • Many farmers and factory workers became unemployed.
Flood protection measures	• The Environment Agency monitors river levels and issues flood warnings to the public, local authorities and the media. • Leaflets have been distributed that explain the flood warnings and tell people what they should do to prepare beforehand. • A scheme called the Eden and Petteril Flood Alleviation Scheme was completed in 2008 — this involved things like building up flood defence walls and levees on the rivers to prevent flooding. • The local council distributes sandbags when flood warnings have been issued.	• Bangladesh has a Flood Forecasting and Warning System (FFWS) with 85 flood monitoring stations. Flood warnings can be issued up to 72 hours before a flood occurs, but the warnings don't reach many rural communities. • There are around 6000 km of man-made levees to prevent flooding in Bangladesh, but they're easily eroded and aren't properly maintained so are often breached by flood waters. They also cause sediment to build up and raise the level of the river bed, making flooding more likely in some places. • Instead of trying to stop flooding entirely, flooding has been allowed in some areas under controlled conditions — called controlled flooding. This means the sediment build-up in channels is reduced, so flooding is less likely.

Flood your mind — with knowledge...

Well, it's pretty clear that floods have different impacts depending on whether they're in an LEDC or an MEDC (because MEDCs have more dosh for protection measures). You need to know two case studies, and it might as well be these.

Revision Summary for Section One

Water load of fun that was. Now it's time to see how much information your brain has soaked up. I think you'll be surprised — I reckon about 16 litres of knowledge has been taken in. Have a go at the questions below and then go back over the section to check your answers. If something's not quite right, pore over the page again. Once you can answer everything correctly you're ready to sail away, sail away, sail away... to the next section.

1) What does the hydrological cycle show?

2) Describe three flows in the hydrological cycle.

3) Describe three stores in the hydrological cycle.

4) What is a drainage basin?

5) Name two outputs from a drainage basin system.

6) What happens at a confluence?

7) Describe freeze-thaw weathering.

8) What is biological weathering?

9) What does a river's long profile show?

10) Describe the cross profile of a river's lower course.

11) What is corrasion?

12) Name two processes of transportation.

13) When does deposition occur?

14) Where do waterfalls form? Name an example.

15) How is a gorge formed?

16) Why do rivers have to wind around interlocking spurs?

17) What is a flood plain?

18) Describe how levees are formed.

19) Name one type of delta and describe what it looks like.

20) Where is the current fastest on a meander?

21) Name the landform created when a meander is cut off by deposition.

22) What do the contour lines on a map show?

23) Give two pieces of map evidence for a waterfall.

24) Give two pieces of map evidence for a river's lower course.

25) Describe three landforms in the valley of a river you have studied.

26) What is river discharge?

27) How does impermeable rock affect river discharge?

28) Describe one physical cause of flooding.

29) Describe one human cause of flooding.

30) Name a hard engineering strategy and describe its benefits.

31) Name a soft engineering strategy and describe its disadvantages.

32) Why are hard engineering strategies usually less sustainable than soft engineering strategies?

33) a) Name a river in an MEDC or an LEDC which has been affected by flooding.

    b) Describe the primary effects of a flood on that river.

    c) Describe two flood protection measures that are used for that river.

Coastal Weathering and Erosion

Weathering is the breakdown of rocks where they are, erosion is when the rocks are broken down and carried away by something, e.g. by seawater. Poor coastal zone, I bet it's worn down.

Rock is Broken Down by Mechanical and Chemical Weathering

1) Mechanical weathering is the breakdown of rock without changing its chemical composition. There's one main type of mechanical weathering that affects coasts — freeze-thaw weathering:

> 1) It happens when the temperature alternates above and below 0 °C (the freezing point of water).
> 2) Water gets into rock that has cracks, e.g. granite.
> 3) When the water freezes it expands, which puts pressure on the rock.
> 4) When the water thaws it contracts, which releases the pressure on the rock.
> 5) Repeated freezing and thawing widens the cracks and causes the rock to break up.

2) Chemical weathering is the breakdown of rock by changing its chemical composition. Carbonation weathering is a type of chemical weathering that happens in warm and wet conditions:

> 1) Rainwater has carbon dioxide dissolved in it, which makes it a weak carbonic acid.
> 2) Carbonic acid reacts with rock that contains calcium carbonate, e.g. carboniferous limestone, so the rocks are dissolved by the rainwater.

Waves Wear Away the Coast using Four Processes of Erosion

> 1) Hydraulic action — waves crash against rock and compress the air in the cracks. This puts pressure on the rock. Repeated compression widens the cracks and makes bits of rock break off.
> 2) Corrasion — eroded particles in the water scrape and rub against rock, removing small pieces.
> 3) Attrition — eroded particles in the water smash into each other and break into smaller fragments. Their edges also get rounded off as they rub together.
> 4) Corrosion — weak carbonic acid in seawater dissolves rock like chalk and limestone.

Destructive Waves Erode the Coastline

Coastlines that are being eroded by destructive waves are called destructive coastlines.

The waves that carry out erosional processes are called destructive waves:

1) Destructive waves have a high frequency (10-14 waves per minute).
2) They're high and steep.
3) Their backwash (the movement of the water back down the beach) is more powerful than their swash (the movement of the water up the beach). This means material is removed from the coast.
4) There are two main factors that affect the size and power of destructive waves, and so how much they erode the coast:

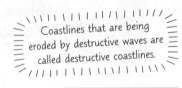

High, steep wave

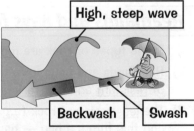

Backwash   Swash

> • Wind — the force of the wind on the water's surface is what creates waves. A strong wind gives large, powerful waves.
> • Fetch — is the distance of water over which the wind has blown to produce a wave. The greater the fetch, the bigger and more powerful the wave.

If you feel like your brain is being eroded — have a little break from revision...

This page is packed full of information, but it's really only about how the coast is worn away and rocks are broken down into smaller pieces. Break your revision down into smaller pieces by learning the processes one at a time.

Coastal Landforms from Erosion

Erosion by waves forms many coastal landforms over long periods of time.

Cliffs Retreat as a Result of Erosion, Weathering and Mass Movements

1) Waves cause most erosion at the foot of a cliff.

2) This forms a wave-cut notch, which is enlarged as erosion continues, making the cliff above the notch unstable.

3) The part of the cliff above sea level is also affected by mechanical and chemical weathering processes. This makes the cliff more unstable and it eventually collapses.

4) The collapsed material is washed away and a new wave-cut notch starts to form.

5) Repeated collapsing results in the cliff retreating.

6) A wave-cut platform is the platform that's left behind as the cliff retreats.

7) The rate of retreat depends on lots of things. For example:

- The geology of the cliff — cliffs formed from soft rock or loose material can retreat very quickly (e.g. several metres a year). Cliffs formed only from hard rock can be eroded over thousands of years.

- Vegetation — cliffs covered in vegetation are more stable, so they're eroded less easily and retreat more slowly.

8) Cliff collapses are mass movements (the shifting of rock and loose material down a slope). They happen when the force of gravity acting on a slope is greater than the force supporting it, e.g. when the notch has made the cliff above unstable.

9) There are three types of mass movement that can affect cliffs:

① Erosion

② Unstable rock
Wave-cut notch

③ Collapsed material

④ New wave-cut notch
Material cleared

There are cliffs and wave-cut platforms at Beachy Head in Sussex.

⑤ Cliff retreats
Wave-cut platform

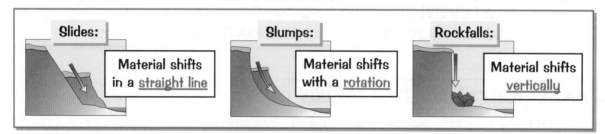

Slides: Material shifts in a straight line

Slumps: Material shifts with a rotation

Rockfalls: Material shifts vertically

Headlands and Bays form where Erosion Resistance is Different

1) Some types of rock are more resistant to erosion than others.

2) Headlands and bays form where there are alternating bands of resistant and less resistant rock along a coast.

3) The less resistant rock (e.g. clay) is eroded quickly and this forms a bay — bays have a gentle slope.

4) The resistant rock (e.g. chalk) is eroded more slowly and it's left jutting out, forming a headland — headlands have steep sides.

5) The Foreland and Swanage Bay in Dorset in the UK are a good example of a headland and a bay.

■ = Resistant rock
□ = Less resistant rock
▷ = Erosion

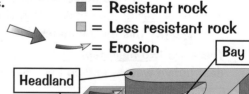

Headland

Bay

What do you call a man with a seagull on his head — Cliff...

If you're one of those people who likes to go right up to the edge of the cliff, perhaps now you'll think twice. There could be an unstable wave-cut notch just below you... not a good way to end your geography career.

Coastal Landforms from Erosion

You're not quite done with <u>coastal erosion</u> yet — it's got a few more tricks up its sleeve...

Headlands <u>are</u> Eroded <u>to form</u> Caves, Arches, Stacks <u>and</u> Stumps

1) Headlands are usually made of <u>resistant rocks</u> (see previous page) that have <u>weaknesses</u> like <u>cracks</u>.

2) <u>Waves</u> crash into the headlands and <u>enlarge</u> the cracks — mainly by <u>hydraulic action</u> and <u>corrasion</u>.

3) <u>Repeated erosion</u> and <u>enlargement</u> of the cracks causes a <u>cave</u> to form.

4) Continued erosion <u>deepens</u> the cave until it <u>breaks through</u> the headland — forming an <u>arch</u>, e.g. Durdle Door in Dorset.

5) Erosion continues to wear away the rock <u>supporting</u> the arch, until it eventually <u>collapses</u>.

6) This forms a <u>stack</u> — an <u>isolated rock</u> that's <u>separate</u> from the headland, e.g. Old Harry in Dorset.

7) The stack is <u>eventually worn away</u> to give a <u>stump</u>, which can be <u>covered</u> by the water at <u>high tide</u>, e.g. Old Harry's Wife in Dorset.

Durdle Door

Old Harry and his Wife

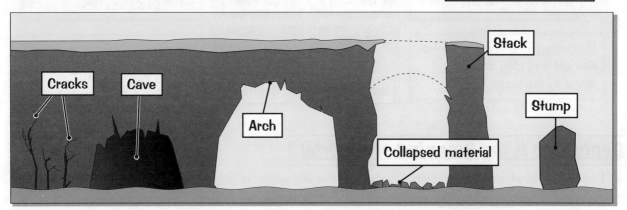

Coves <u>Form where there are</u> Parallel Bands <u>of</u> Hard <u>and</u> Soft Rock

1) A <u>cove</u> is a <u>wide</u>, <u>circular bay</u> with a <u>narrow entrance</u>.

2) They form where there's a <u>band of hard rock</u> (e.g. limestone) <u>along a coast</u> with a band of <u>softer</u> rock <u>behind</u> it (e.g. clay).

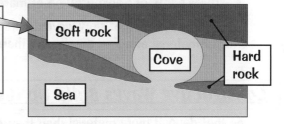

3) Where there's a <u>weakness</u> in the band of hard rock a <u>narrow gap</u> will be eroded. The softer rock behind will then be <u>eroded much more</u> to form the cove.

4) <u>Lulworth Cove</u> in <u>Dorset</u> is a good example.

Lulworth Cove

I'm feeling slightly stumped about all these coastal landforms...

<u>Crack erosion</u> — sounds painful. If you don't want it to happen to you, then don't stand in the sea for too many years in a row. Just a few <u>landforms</u> to learn here, and as ever, learning the diagrams will help in the exam.

Coastal Transportation and Deposition

The <u>material</u> that's been <u>eroded</u> is <u>moved around</u> the coast and <u>deposited</u> by waves.

Transportation is the Movement of Material

Material is transported <u>along coasts</u> by a process called <u>longshore drift</u>:

1) <u>Waves</u> follow the <u>direction</u> of the <u>prevailing</u> (most common) <u>wind</u>.

2) They usually hit the coast at an <u>oblique angle</u> (any angle that <u>isn't a right angle</u>).

3) The <u>swash</u> carries material <u>up the beach</u>, in the <u>same direction as the waves</u>.

4) The <u>backwash</u> then carries material <u>down the beach</u> at <u>right angles</u>, back towards the sea.

5) Over time, material <u>zigzags</u> along the coast.

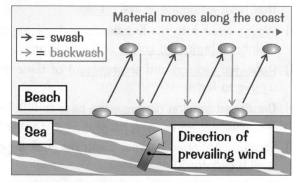

There are <u>four</u> other <u>processes of transportation</u> that you need to know about:

<u>Traction</u> — <u>large</u> particles like boulders are <u>pushed</u> along the <u>sea bed</u> by the <u>force of the water</u>.

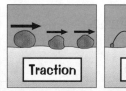

<u>Saltation</u> — <u>pebble-sized</u> particles are <u>bounced</u> along the <u>sea bed</u> by the <u>force of the water</u>.

<u>Suspension</u> — <u>small</u> particles like silt and clay are <u>carried</u> along in the water.

<u>Solution</u> — <u>soluble materials</u> dissolve in the water and are <u>carried</u> along.

Deposition is the Dropping of Material

1) Deposition is when <u>material</u> being <u>carried</u> by the sea water is <u>dropped on the coast</u>.

2) Coasts are <u>built up</u> when the <u>amount of deposition</u> is <u>greater</u> than the <u>amount of erosion</u>.

3) The <u>amount of material</u> that's <u>deposited</u> on an area of coast is <u>increased</u> when:

- There's <u>lots of erosion</u> elsewhere on the coast, so there's <u>lots of material available</u>.
- There's <u>lots</u> of <u>transportation</u> of material <u>into</u> the area.

4) <u>Low energy</u> waves (i.e. <u>slow</u> waves) carry material to the coast but they're <u>not strong enough</u> to take a lot of material away — this means there's <u>lots of deposition</u> and <u>very little erosion</u>.

Constructive Waves Build Up the Coastline

Waves that <u>deposit more material</u> than they <u>erode</u> and build up the coast are called <u>constructive waves</u>.

Coastlines being built up by constructive waves are called constructive coastlines.

1) Constructive waves have a <u>low frequency</u> (6-8 waves per minute).

2) They're <u>low</u> and <u>long</u>.

3) The <u>swash</u> is <u>powerful</u> and it <u>carries material up the coast</u>.

4) The backwash is <u>weaker</u> and it <u>doesn't</u> take a lot of material <u>back down the coast</u>. This means material is <u>deposited</u> on the coast.

5) Constructive waves are made by <u>weaker winds</u> and have a <u>shorter fetch</u> than destructive waves.

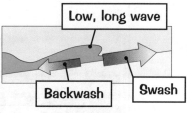

Why did the constructive wave go to the bank? It wanted to make a deposit...

Some more processes to learn here but none of them are tricky. You might find it useful to draw yourself a <u>diagram</u> of how <u>longshore drift</u> works — you'll get a feel for how the material is <u>moved along</u> the coast in a <u>zigzag</u> pattern.

Section Two — Coasts

Coastal Landforms from Deposition

Here are some more exciting <u>landforms</u> for you to learn about. This time it's all about <u>deposition</u>. Unfortunately you're going to be slightly disappointed — sandcastles won't be in the exam.

Beaches are formed by Deposition

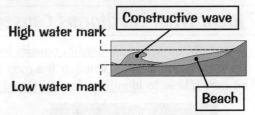

1) Beaches are found on coasts <u>between</u> the <u>high water mark</u> (the <u>highest point on the land</u> the <u>sea level</u> gets to) and the <u>low water mark</u> (the <u>lowest point</u> on the land the <u>sea level</u> gets to).

2) They're formed by <u>constructive waves</u> (see previous page) depositing material like <u>sand</u> and <u>shingle</u>.

3) <u>Sand</u> and <u>shingle beaches</u> have different <u>characteristics</u>:

- <u>Sand</u> beaches are <u>flat</u> and <u>wide</u> — sand particles are <u>small</u> and the weak backwash <u>can</u> move them <u>back down</u> the beach, creating a <u>long</u>, <u>gentle slope</u>.
- <u>Shingle</u> beaches are <u>steep</u> and <u>narrow</u> — shingle particles are <u>large</u> and the weak backwash <u>can't</u> move them back down the beach. The shingle particles <u>build up</u> and create a <u>steep slope</u>.

Spits and Bars are formed by Longshore Drift

Spits are just <u>beaches</u> that <u>stick out</u> into the sea — they're <u>joined</u> to the coast at <u>one end</u>. If a spit sticks out so far that it <u>connects</u> with another bit of the mainland, it'll form a <u>bar</u>. Spits and bars are formed by the process of <u>longshore drift</u> (see previous page).

SPITS

1) Spits form at <u>sharp bends</u> in the coastline, e.g. at a <u>river mouth</u>.
2) <u>Longshore drift</u> transports sand and shingle <u>past</u> the bend and <u>deposits</u> it in the sea.
3) Strong winds and waves can <u>curve</u> the end of the spit (forming a <u>recurved end</u>).
4) The <u>sheltered area</u> behind the spit is <u>protected from waves</u> — lots of material <u>accumulates</u> in this area, which means <u>plants</u> can grow there.
5) <u>Over time</u>, the sheltered area can become a <u>mud flat</u> or a <u>salt marsh</u>.

An example of a spit is Spurn Head in Yorkshire.

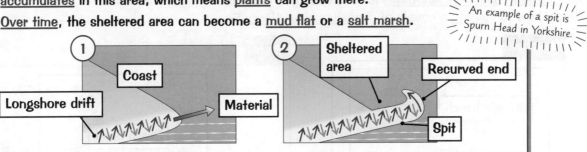

BARS

1) A bar is formed when a spit <u>joins two headlands together</u>, e.g. there's a bar at Slapton in Devon.
2) The bar <u>cuts off</u> the bay between the headlands <u>from the sea</u>.
3) This means a <u>lagoon</u> can form <u>behind</u> the bar.
4) A bar that <u>connects</u> the <u>shore</u> to an <u>island</u> (often a <u>stack</u>) is called a <u>tombolo</u>. For example, <u>Chesil Beach</u> in Dorset joins to the <u>Isle of Portland</u>.

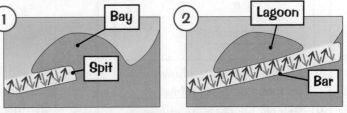

Depositional bars — the only cocktail they serve is a long beach iced tea...

The things you learn in geography are life skills. If you have to meet someone at the <u>beach</u> you now know exactly where to stand — between the <u>high</u> and <u>low water marks</u>, of course. And who said geography was just about maps...

Coastal Landforms on Maps

I love <u>maps</u>, all geographers love maps. I can't get to sleep unless I've got one under my pillow. So I'm going to do you a favour and share my passion with you — check out these <u>coastal landforms</u>...

Identifying Landforms Caused by Erosion

You might be asked to <u>identify coastal landforms</u> on a <u>map</u> in the exam. The simplest thing they could ask is whether the map is showing <u>erosional</u> or <u>depositional landforms</u>, so here's how to <u>identify</u> a few <u>erosional landforms</u> to get you started:

Have a gander at pages 103-104 for more on reading maps.

Caves, arches and stacks

1) <u>Caves</u> and <u>arches can't be seen</u> on a map because of the rock <u>above them</u>.

2) <u>Stacks</u> look like <u>little blobs</u> in the sea.

Cliffs and wave-cut platforms

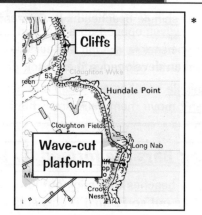

1) <u>Cliffs</u> (and other steep slopes) are shown on maps as <u>little black lines</u>.

2) <u>Wave-cut platforms</u> are shown as <u>bumpy edges</u> along the coast.

Identifying Landforms Caused by Deposition

<u>Identifying depositional landforms</u> is easy once you know that <u>beaches</u> are shown in <u>yellow</u> on maps. Here's how to <u>identify</u> a couple of <u>depositional landforms</u>:

Beaches

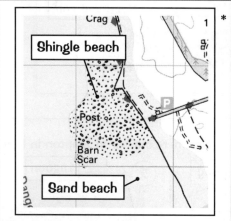

1) <u>Sand beaches</u> are shown on maps as <u>pale yellow</u>.

2) <u>Shingle beaches</u> are shown as <u>white</u> or <u>yellow</u> with <u>speckles</u>.

Spits

1) <u>Spits</u> are shown by a <u>beach</u> that carries on <u>out to sea</u>, but is still <u>attached</u> to the land at <u>one end</u>.

2) There might also be a <u>sharp bend</u> in the coast that caused it to form (see p. 21).

Find the spit on the map — and then wipe it off...

There are some seriously easy marks up for grabs with map questions so make sure you learn this page. You could practise looking for <u>landforms</u> on any <u>maps</u> you can get a hold of. Probably best to avoid the inner-city maps though.

Section Two — Coasts

Coastal Area — Case Study

If <u>coastal landforms</u> are your thing (and let's face it, how could they not be), then the <u>Dorset coast</u> is paradise on Earth. It's got the lot — <u>headlands</u>, <u>bays</u>, <u>arches</u>, <u>stacks</u>, <u>coves</u>, <u>tombolos</u>, <u>lagoons</u>...

The Dorset Coast has Examples of many Coastal Landforms

The Dorset coast is made from bands of <u>hard rock</u> (like limestone and chalk) and <u>soft rock</u> (like clay). The rocks have been <u>eroded at different rates</u> giving <u>headlands</u> and <u>bays</u> and lots of other exciting coastal landforms.

Durdle Door

<u>Durdle Door</u> is a great example of an <u>arch</u>. <u>Erosion by waves</u> opened up a <u>crack</u> in the limestone <u>headland</u>, which became a <u>cave</u> and then developed into an arch.

Lulworth Cove

<u>Lulworth Cove</u> is a cove formed after a gap was eroded in a <u>band of limestone</u>. Behind the limestone is a band of <u>clay</u>, which has been eroded away to form the <u>cove</u>. The same is now starting to happen at <u>Stair Hole</u> further west along the coast.

©iStockphoto.com/Leslie Budzynski

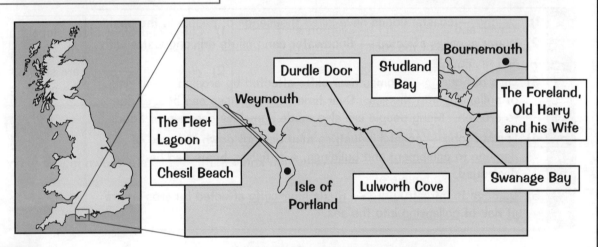

The Fleet Lagoon

Chesil Beach

Weymouth

Durdle Door

Isle of Portland

Lulworth Cove

Studland Bay

Bournemouth

The Foreland, Old Harry and his Wife

Swanage Bay

Chesil Beach

<u>Chesil Beach</u> is a <u>tombolo</u> formed by <u>longshore drift</u>. It joins the <u>Isle of Portland</u> to the mainland. Behind Chesil Beach is a shallow <u>lagoon</u> called <u>The Fleet Lagoon</u>.

©iStockphoto.com/IAN WATT

Swanage Bay and Studland Bay

There are two <u>bays</u> with beaches called <u>Swanage Bay</u> and <u>Studland Bay</u>. They're areas of <u>softer rock</u> (<u>sandstone</u> and <u>clay</u>). In between them is a <u>headland</u> called <u>The Foreland</u> made from a band of <u>harder rock</u> (<u>chalk</u>). The end of the headland has been eroded to become a <u>stack</u> called <u>Old Harry</u> and a <u>stump</u> called <u>Old Harry's Wife</u>.

©iStockphoto.com/Glen Rodgers

I love a good tombolo — prizes and fun for everyone...

That's actually Old Harry's <u>second wife</u>. His first wife <u>collapsed</u> into the sea in 1896. It was sad, but she would've wanted him to move on. Before you move on, make sure you know the <u>names</u> of the <u>landforms</u> of the Dorset coast.

Page 24

Reasons for Protecting Coastlines

Coastal areas are at risk from erosion and flooding by the sea. Both can cause a lot of problems for the environment and the people living there. So there's lots of reasons why coastlines need to be protected.

There are Human Reasons to Protect Coastlines

Human reasons to protect coastlines from flooding and erosion can be divided into economic and social factors:

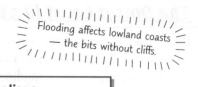
Flooding affects lowland coasts — the bits without cliffs.

Economic

1) Loss of tourism — many coastal areas are popular tourist destinations. Flooding and erosion can put people off visiting. Fewer tourists means businesses that rely on tourism may close.

2) Businesses near cliffs that are eroding are at risk of collapsing into the sea. Coastal flooding can damage or destroy business premises. Businesses have to relocate, make costly repairs or can be forced to shut down.

3) Coastal flooding damages agricultural land because seawater has a high salt content. Salt reduces soil fertility, and so crop production can be affected for years after a flood. Farmland is also lost to coastal erosion, which has a huge effect on farmers' livelihoods.

4) Property prices can fall if houses are affected by flooding or are at risk from erosion. People may also be unable to get their properties insured.

Social

1) Deaths — coastal floods have killed thousands of people in the past.

2) Water supplies affected — floodwater can pollute drinking water with salt or sewage.

3) Loss of housing — homes near cliffs affected by erosion are at risk of collapsing into the sea. Over time whole villages can be lost due to erosion. Many people are also made homeless because of floods.

4) Loss of jobs — coastal industries may be shut down because of damage to equipment and buildings, e.g. fishing boats can be destroyed.

5) Damage to infrastructure — roads near cliffs affected by erosion are at risk of collapsing into the sea.

Protect the coastline. Sir, yes sir!

There are also Environmental Reasons to Protect Coastlines

Environmental reasons to protect coastlines from flooding and erosion can be divided into... OK, just environmental factors.

Environmental

1) Ecosystems affected — seawater has a high salt content. Increased salt levels due to coastal flooding can damage or kill organisms in an ecosystem. The force of floodwater also uproots trees and plants, and standing floodwater drowns some trees and plants.

2) Some SSSIs (Sites of Special Scientific Interest) are threatened by coastal erosion. E.g. the Lagoons on the Holderness coast in east Yorkshire are part of an SSSI. The Lagoons are separated from the sea by a narrow strip of sand and shingle (a bar). If this is eroded it will connect the Lagoons to the sea and they would be destroyed.

Coastline protection for me means sunglasses, sunscreen and a shark detector...

It's no fun living near the sea if you're going to be flooded any moment or if your house is going to fall into the sea. No amount of ice cream or donkey rides can comfort you if you lose your home and job due to erosion or flooding.

Section Two — Coasts

Coastal Management Strategies

The <u>aim</u> of coastal management is to <u>protect</u> people and the environment from the <u>impacts</u> of erosion and flooding. Unfortunately it's not as simple as a big fence and a bucket, nice though that would be.

Coastal Defences Include Hard and Soft Engineering

There are <u>two</u> types of strategy to <u>deal with coastal flooding</u> and <u>erosion</u>:

<u>Hard engineering</u> — <u>man-made structures</u> built to <u>control the flow</u> of the sea and <u>reduce flooding</u> and <u>erosion</u>.

<u>Soft engineering</u> — schemes set up using <u>knowledge</u> of the sea and its <u>processes</u> to <u>reduce the effects of flooding</u> and <u>erosion</u>.

	Strategy	What it is	Benefits	Disadvantages
HARD ENGINEERING	Sea wall	A <u>wall</u> made out of a <u>hard material</u> like concrete that <u>reflects waves</u> back to sea.	It <u>prevents erosion</u> of the coast. It also acts as a <u>barrier</u> to <u>prevent flooding</u>.	It creates a <u>strong backwash</u>, which <u>erodes under</u> the wall. Sea walls are <u>very expensive</u> to <u>build</u> and to <u>maintain</u>.
	Rip rap	<u>Boulders</u> that are <u>piled up</u> along the coast.	The boulders <u>absorb wave energy</u> and so <u>reduce erosion</u> and <u>flooding</u>.	Boulders can be <u>moved around</u> by <u>strong waves</u>, so they need to be <u>replaced</u>.
	Groynes	Wooden or stone <u>fences</u> that are built at <u>right angles</u> to the coast. They <u>trap material</u> transported by <u>longshore drift</u>.	Groynes create <u>wider beaches</u> which <u>slow</u> the <u>waves</u>. This gives greater <u>protection</u> from <u>flooding</u> and <u>erosion</u>.	They <u>starve beaches</u> further down the coast of sand, making them <u>narrower</u>. Narrower beaches <u>don't protect</u> the coast as well, leading to <u>greater erosion</u> and <u>floods</u>.
	Revetments	<u>Slanted structures</u> made of concrete, wood or rocks built at the <u>foot of cliffs</u>.	They <u>absorb wave energy</u> and so <u>reduce erosion</u>.	<u>Expensive</u> to build and they create a strong backwash that <u>erodes</u> under the barrier.
	Gabions	<u>Rock-filled cages</u>, built at the <u>foot of cliffs</u>.	They <u>absorb wave energy</u> and so <u>reduce erosion</u>.	They look <u>ugly</u>.
	Breakwaters	Concrete <u>blocks</u> or <u>boulders</u> deposited on the sea bed <u>off the coast</u>.	They force waves to <u>break offshore</u> so their erosive power is <u>reduced</u> before they reach the shore.	They're <u>expensive</u> and can be <u>damaged</u> by storms.
SOFT ENGINEERING	Beach replenishment	Sand and shingle from <u>elsewhere</u> (e.g. the <u>offshore seabed</u>) that's <u>added</u> to beaches.	Beach replenishment creates <u>wider beaches</u> which <u>slow</u> the <u>waves</u>. This gives greater <u>protection</u> from <u>flooding</u> and <u>erosion</u>.	Taking <u>material</u> from the <u>seabed</u> can <u>kill</u> organisms like <u>sponges</u> and <u>corals</u>. It's a <u>very expensive</u> defence. It has to be <u>repeated</u>.
	Managed retreat	<u>Removing</u> an <u>existing defence</u> and allowing the land behind it to <u>flood</u>.	<u>Over time</u> the land will become <u>marshland</u> — creating <u>new habitats</u>. <u>Flooding</u> and <u>erosion</u> are <u>reduced</u> behind the marshland. It's a fairly <u>cheap</u> defence.	People may <u>disagree</u> over what land is <u>allowed to flood</u>, e.g. flooding farmland would affect the <u>livelihood</u> of farmers.

Some strategies for <u>coastal management</u> are <u>more sustainable than others</u>. Sustainable strategies meet the <u>needs</u> of <u>people today</u> (i.e. they <u>reduce flooding</u> and <u>erosion</u>), <u>without stopping people in the future</u> getting the things they <u>need</u>. This means <u>not using up too many resources</u> (e.g. money) or <u>damaging the environment</u>.

Hard engineering strategies are usually <u>less sustainable</u> than soft engineering strategies because they generally <u>cost more money to build and maintain</u>, and they <u>damage the environment more</u>.

A good management strategy involves warm-ups — they reduce groyne strains...

Wow, that sure is a mighty fine table. It seems like a lot to remember but I promise you, it's really not that tough. Make sure you know at least a couple of <u>benefits</u> and <u>disadvantages</u> for <u>each strategy</u> so you'll be a winner in the exam.

Coastal Management — Case Study

Holderness in east Yorkshire has one of the fastest eroding coastlines in Europe. What a claim to fame...

Hard Engineering Strategies have been used Along Holderness

There's rapid erosion along the Holderness coast (about 1.8m per year), which has had lots of impacts:

1) Homes near the cliffs (e.g. in Skipsea) are at risk of collapsing into the sea.

2) Businesses are at risk from erosion so people will lose their jobs, e.g. Seaside Caravan Park at Ulrome is losing an average of 10 pitches a year.

3) The gas terminal at Easington is at risk (it's only 25 m from the cliff edge). This terminal accounts for 25% of Britain's gas supply.

4) 80 000 m² of farmland is lost each year. This has a huge effect on farmers' livelihoods.

To try to reduce these effects, 11.4 km of Holderness coastline has been protected by hard engineering:

Bridlington is protected from erosion and flooding by a 4.7 km long sea wall as well as wooden groynes.

There's a sea wall, wooden groynes and rip rap at Hornsea to protect the village from erosion and flooding.

There are groynes to create wider beaches and a sea wall at Withernsea. Some rip rap was placed in front of the wall after it was damaged in severe storms in 1992.

Defences including two rock groynes were built at Mappleton in 1991. They cost £2 million and were built to protect the village and a coastal road from erosion and flooding.

The eastern side of Spurn Head is protected by groynes and rip rap. This also protects the Humber Estuary behind Spurn Head.

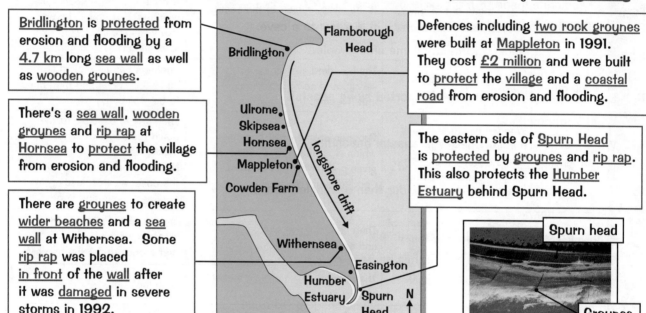

UNIVERSITY OF CAMBRIDGE AIR PHOTOGRAPHS / SCIENCE PHOTO LIBRARY

The Strategies are Locally Successful but Cause Problems Elsewhere

1) Groynes protect local areas but cause narrow beaches to form further down the Holderness coast. This increases erosion down the coast, e.g. Cowden Farm (south of Mappleton) is now at risk of falling into the sea.

2) The material produced from the erosion of Holderness is normally transported south into the Humber Estuary and down the Lincolnshire coast. Reducing the amount of material that's eroded and transported south increases the risk of flooding in the Humber Estuary, because there's less material to slow the floodwater down.

3) The rate of coastal retreat along the Lincolnshire coast is also increased, because less new material is being added.

4) Spurn Head is at risk of being eroded away because less material is being added to it.

5) Bays are forming between the protected areas, and the protected areas are becoming headlands which are being eroded more heavily. This means maintaining the defences in the protected areas is becoming more expensive.

> Strategies that benefit some areas but cause problems in other areas can lead to conflict.

Holderness coastal management officer — probably not the easiest job to have...

Maybe you don't love case studies as much as me (I mean, how could you), but they really have to be learnt. It's always a speedy route to impressing the examiner — and a happy examiner makes for a more pleasant results day.

Section Two — Coasts

Revision Summary for Section Two

So, you've coasted through another section — that means it's time to find out just how much of this information has been deposited in your noggin. Have a go at the questions below. If you're finding it tough, just look back at the pages in the section and then have another go. You'll be ready to move on to the next section when you can answer all of these questions without breaking sweat.

1)   What is mechanical weathering?

2)   Describe the process of chemical weathering.

3)   How do waves erode the coast by hydraulic action?

4)   What waves are associated with coastal erosion?

5)   Describe how a wave-cut platform is formed.

6)   Give an example of one type of mass movement.

7)   Are headlands made of more or less resistant rock?

8)   Describe how erosion can turn a crack in a cliff into a cave.

9)   Explain how a stack is formed. Name an example.

10) What is a cove?

11) By what process is material transported along coasts?

12) What is deposition?

13) What waves are associated with coastal deposition?

14) Where is a beach formed on a coast?

15) Why is a sand beach flatter and wider than a shingle beach?

16) What is a bar?

17) Where do spits form? Name an example.

18) Why can't cracks, caves and arches be seen on a map?

19) How are cliffs shown on a map?

20) On maps, what do speckles on top of yellow shading tell you?

21) a) Name a coastal area you have studied which has erosional and depositional landforms.

     b) Name one erosional landform in that area.

     c) Name one depositional landform in that area.

22) Give two economic impacts of coastal flooding and erosion.

23) Give two social impacts of coastal flooding and erosion.

24) Describe the difference between hard engineering and soft engineering coastal management strategies.

25) Explain a disadvantage of using groynes as a coastal defence.

26) a) Name two soft engineering strategies.

     b) Give one benefit of each strategy.

27) a) Describe three impacts erosion has had on a coastal area you have studied.

     b) Give two examples of hard engineering strategies used on the same coastline.

     c) Describe two problems caused by the use of hard engineering strategies on this coastline.

Population Growth

The population change section — putting the 'pop' in 'popular'. Studying population change is amazing —
you'd have to be stark raving mad not to agree with me. Only one way to judge for yourself though...

The World's Population is Growing Rapidly

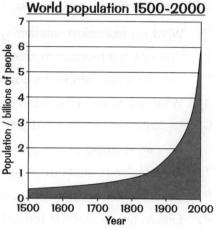

World population 1500-2000

1) The graph shows world population for the years 1500-2000
   — it's been increasing and is still increasing today.

2) The population of the world is increasing all the time and
   the rate it's increasing at is getting faster and faster.

3) There are two things that affect the population size of the world:

> Birth rate — the number of live babies born per
> thousand of the population per year.
>
> Death rate — the number of deaths per thousand
> of the population per year.

4) When the birth rate is higher than the death rate, more people
   are being born than are dying, so the population grows — this is called the natural increase.

5) It's called the natural decrease when the death rate's higher than the birth rate.

6) The population size of a country is also affected by migration — the movement of people
   from one area to another area (see p. 35).

Countries go Through Five Stages of Population Growth

1) Birth rates and death rates differ from country to country.
   This means that population growth is faster in some countries than others.

2) Population growth also changes within a country over time (it can get faster or slower).

3) Countries go through five different stages of population growth.

4) These stages are shown by the Demographic Transition Model (DTM):

	Stage 1	Stage 2	Stage 3	Stage 4	Stage 5
Birth rate	High and fluctuating	High and steady	Rapidly falling	Low and fluctuating	Slowly falling
Death rate	High and fluctuating	Rapidly falling	Slowly falling	Low and fluctuating	Low and steady
Population growth rate	Zero	Very high	High	Zero	Negative
Population size	Low and steady	Rapidly increasing	Increasing	High and steady	Slowly falling
Example countries	No countries, some tribes in Brazil	Gambia	Egypt	UK, USA	Japan

You know what — this world population is growing on me...

DTM — it stands for Done Too Much (work that is). Sigh, it's a pretty useful thing to know though — it pops up all
over the place, so you should really learn it. I know it's no Kate Moss, but it's not bad for a geography model.

Population Growth and Structure

The population fun's not over yet — you've still got 10 pages to go and the exciting worlds of population pyramids, overpopulation and ageing populations to cover. And then there's migration. I could just pee I'm so excited.

Population Growth is Linked to How Developed a Country is

1) As countries become more developed, birth and death rates change, which affects the population growth. E.g. as a country develops healthcare improves, which leads to a drop in death rate and faster population growth.

2) So as countries become more developed the population changes and the country moves through the stages of the DTM.

3) This means Less Economically Developed Countries (LEDCs) are in the earlier stages of the DTM (2-3) — population growth rate is high because birth rates are high and death rates are beginning to fall.

4) More Economically Developed Countries (MEDCs) are in the later stages of the DTM (4-5) — they usually have low or negative population growth because birth rates and death rates are low.

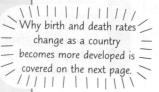
Why birth and death rates change as a country becomes more developed is covered on the next page.

A Country's Population Structure Changes as it Develops

The population structure of a country is how many people there are of each age group in the population, and how many there are of each sex. Population structure is shown using population pyramids. Population structure differs from country to country and it changes as countries become more developed. But before you get into the details, you need to understand population pyramids. You can learn a lot about a country from its population pyramid. For example:

1 The higher the top bar on the pyramid, the better the life expectancy (the average age in years a person can expect to live). E.g. in the country shown in the pyramid some people are living to 100, so life expectancy will be quite high.

2 You can see if there are an equal number of men and women, and if they live to a similar age — the gender balance of the country. E.g. in the country shown in the pyramid, women are living longer than men.

If you have to sketch a pyramid just draw the outline shape, not the individual bars.

3 Sometimes pyramids have bulges or dips in them. This happens when lots of a particular age group move into or out of the country, or are killed in a war.

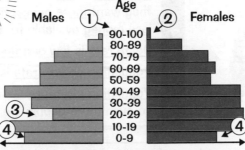

Population pyramid

Age

Males ①→ ② Females

90-100
80-89
70-79
60-69
50-59
40-49
30-39
20-29
10-19
0-9

③→ ④→ ← ④

Number of people

4 The 0-9 age group tells you about birth rate. E.g. there are fewer people aged 0-9 because the birth rate has decreased over the last 10 years.

Pyramids can have different age categories, e.g. 5 year intervals instead of 10 year intervals. Pyramids with 5 year intervals can be used to work out the dependency ratio (how many people are supported by the working population) — it's the number of people aged 0-15 plus the number of people aged 65 and over, divided by the number of people aged 16-64.

Population data comes from lots of sources, e.g. censuses and birth certificates.

Population pyramids — no-one knows how the ancient people built them...

I've not been to Egypt, but that population pyramid doesn't look like a pyramid to me. It's all dumpy, like it's suffering from pyramid muffin tops. Oh well, you need to learn what they are, whether they're pyramid shaped or not.

Population Growth and Structure

I've never seen so many pyramids in all my life. There's fat and thin, but none made of chocolate and nuts.

There are Many Reasons Why Population Growth and Structure Change

As a country develops and moves through the stages of the DTM its birth and death rates change. This causes the population growth rate, structure and pyramid to change too:

DEVELOPMENT

Stage 1

Birth rate is high because there's no use of contraception, and people have lots of children because many infants die.

Death rate is high due to poor healthcare or famine.

Population growth rate is zero.

Population structure — life expectancy is low (few people reach old age), so the population is made up of mostly young people.

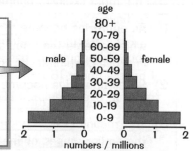

Stage 2

Birth rate is high because there's no use of contraception. Also, the economy is based on agriculture so people have lots of children to work on farms.

Death rate falls due to improved healthcare and diet.

Population growth rate is very high.

Population structure — life expectancy has increased, but there are still more young people than older people.

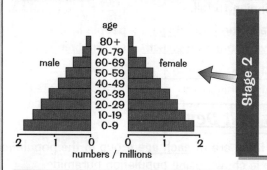

Stage 3

Birth rate is rapidly falling as women have a more equal place in society and better education. The use of contraception increases and more women work instead of having children. The economy also changes to manufacturing, so fewer children are needed to work on farms.

Death rate falls due to more medical advances.

Population growth rate is high.

Population structure — more people are living to be older.

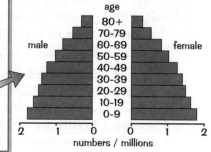

Stage 4

Birth rate is low — people's wealth improves and they want more possessions. This means there's less money available for having children.

Death rate is low and fluctuating.

Population growth rate is zero.

Population structure — life expectancy is high, so even more people are living to be older.

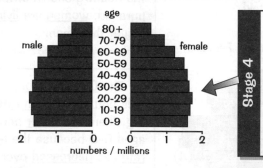

Stage 5

Birth rate is slowly falling — there's less money available to raise children because people have dependent elderly relatives.

Death rate is low and fluctuating.

Population growth rate is negative.

Population structure — more older people than young people.

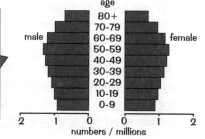

So the Egyptians weren't actually a very developed civilisation...

There are a fair few words on this page but they're all important. You need to know the reasons why birth rate, death rate, population growth and population structure change as countries become more developed.

Overpopulation

It's not always a case of 'the more the merrier' — rapid population growth can lead to overpopulation.

Overpopulation is When There are Too Many People for the Resources

1) Overpopulation is usually caused by rapid population growth.

2) So it's most likely to happen in LEDCs (such as Gambia) in Stages 2 and 3 of the DTM. They have a high birth rate and a falling death rate, causing a high population growth rate.

3) Low life expectancy together with a high birth rate also leads to a youthful population. A youthful population has a high dependency ratio (see p. 29) — there are lots of people under 15 that are dependent on the working population (aged 15–64).

MEDCs can be overpopulated too.

4) Youthful, overpopulated LEDCs face many social, economic and environmental problems:

SOCIAL

1) Services like healthcare and education can't cope with the large, young population, so not everybody has access to them.

2) Children have to work to help support their large families, so they miss out on education.

3) There aren't enough houses for everyone, so people are forced to live in makeshift houses in overcrowded settlements. This leads to health problems because the houses aren't always connected to sewers and they don't always have access to clean water.

4) There are food shortages if the country can't grow or import enough food for the population.

ECONOMIC

1) There aren't enough jobs for the number of people in the country, so unemployment increases.

2) There's increased poverty because more people are born into families that are already poor.

ENVIRONMENTAL

Increased waste and pollution, e.g. more cars will release more greenhouse gases, and more waste will need to go to landfill sites.
More natural resources are used up, e.g. more trees are chopped down for firewood.

There are Different Strategies to Control Overpopulation

Countries need to control rapid population growth so they don't become overpopulated. They also need to develop in a way that's sustainable. This means developing in a way that allows people today to get the things they need, but without stopping people in the future from getting what they need. Here are a couple of examples of population policies and how they help to achieve sustainable development:

Birth control programmes

Birth control programmes aim to reduce the birth rate.
Some governments do this by having laws about how many children couples are allowed to have (see next page). Governments also help couples to plan (and limit) how many children they have by offering free contraception and sex education.

How babies are made

This helps towards sustainable development because it means the population won't get much bigger. There won't be many more people using up resources today, so there will be some left for future generations.

Immigration laws

Immigration laws aim to control immigration (people moving to a country to live there permanently). Governments can limit the number of people that are allowed to immigrate (see p. 36).
They can also be selective about who they let in, e.g. letting in fewer people of child-bearing age means there will be fewer immigrants having children. This helps towards sustainable development because it slows down population growth rate.

When it comes to overpopulation I blame the parents...

If you're not living on the edge, you're taking up too much room — sound advice for people in overpopulated countries. You need to learn the strategies to control population growth and how these relate to sustainable development.

Managing Overpopulation — Case Study

Natural population increase in China is causing lots of problems (including too many stinky nappies).

China has the World's Largest Population

1) China has the largest population of any country in the world — over 1.3 billion.

2) In 1949 the population was only 540 million so families were encouraged to have more children to help produce more food and build a strong army.

3) By 1970 the population had increased to 830 million but China's resources couldn't cope — there was a disastrous famine from 1958–1961 and lots of people had no access to things like water and electricity.

The Late, Long and Few Policy was Introduced in 1970

1) The 'late, long, few' policy (1970-79) aimed to reduce the natural population growth by encouraging people to have children later, leave longer gaps between each child, and to have fewer children in total.

2) The policy worked well — the fertility rate fell sharply from 5.7 in 1970 to 2.9 in 1979.

3) This policy helped to make development in China more sustainable by reducing the rapid growth of the population. This meant that resources weren't used up as quickly and less waste was produced than if the population had continued growing rapidly.

Fertility rate is the average number of children a woman has in her lifetime.

4) But the population was still growing, so China came up with a new policy...

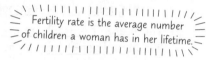

PRAMS 'R' US
CLOSING DOWN SALE

The One-Child Policy came into Force in 1979

1) The 'one-child policy' was introduced in 1979 and encourages people to have only one child.

2) Couples that only have one child are given benefits like longer maternity leave, better housing and free education for the child. Couples that have more than one child don't get any benefits and are also fined part of their income.

Effectiveness

1) The policy has prevented up to 400 million births. The fertility rate has dropped from 2.9 in 1979 to around 1.8 in 2009.

2) Some people think that it wasn't just the one-child policy that slowed population growth. They say the late, long, few policy was more effective, and that Chinese people want fewer children anyway as they've become more wealthy.

3) China's one-child policy helps towards sustainable development — the population hasn't grown as fast (and got as big) as it would have done without the policy, so fewer resources have been used.

4) But the policy has also meant that China has an ageing population — there's a lower proportion of young people compared to older people, which can cause other problems (see the next page).

5) Over the years, the policy has changed so there are some exceptions:

- In some rural areas, couples are allowed to have a second child if the first is a girl, or has a physical disability. This is because more children are still needed to work on farms in rural areas.

- If one of the parents has a disability or if both parents are only children, then couples are allowed to have a second child. This is so there are enough people to look after the parents.

Someone should tell the pandas they can have as many babies as they like...

The Chinese government has taken pretty drastic action — just think of all those only children with no siblings to torment. But it's worked — China's population is now predicted to peak in 2030 and then start dropping.

Ageing Populations

You've already seen how youthful populations can cause problems. Well, ageing populations can face <u>economic</u> and <u>social</u> problems too. They also tend to consume a high quantity of teacakes.

An *Ageing* Population has *Social* and *Economic* Impacts

The <u>population structure</u> of an ageing population has <u>more older</u> people (over 65) than <u>younger</u> people because <u>few</u> people are being <u>born</u>, and <u>more</u> people are <u>surviving</u> to old age. Countries with an ageing population are usually the <u>richer countries</u> in Stage <u>5</u> of the <u>DTM</u> (see p. 28).

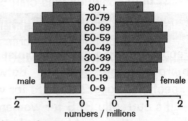

Older people are <u>supported</u> by the <u>working population</u> (aged 16-64) — they're <u>dependent</u> on them. So in a country with an ageing population there's a <u>higher proportion</u> of people who are dependent. This has <u>social</u> and <u>economic impacts</u>:

SOCIAL

1) <u>Healthcare services</u> are <u>stretched more</u> because older people need more medical care.

2) People will need to spend more time working as <u>unpaid carers</u> for older family members. This means that the working population have <u>less leisure time</u> and are <u>more stressed</u> and <u>worried</u>.

3) People may have <u>fewer children</u> because they <u>can't afford</u> lots of children when they have dependent older relatives. This leads to a <u>drop in birth rate</u>.

4) The <u>more</u> old people there are, the <u>lower</u> the <u>pension</u> provided by the government will be. People will have to <u>retire later</u> because they <u>can't afford</u> to get by on a state pension.

ECONOMIC

1) The working population <u>pay taxes</u>, some of which the government use to pay the <u>state pensions</u> of older people, and to pay for <u>services</u> like retirement homes and healthcare. Taxes would need to <u>go up</u> because there are <u>more pensions</u> to pay for, and older people need <u>more healthcare</u>.

2) The <u>economy</u> of the country would <u>grow more slowly</u> — <u>less money</u> is being spent on things that help the economy to <u>grow</u>, e.g. education and business, and <u>more money</u> is being spent on things that <u>don't</u> help the economy to grow, e.g. retirement homes.

There are *Different Strategies* to *Cope* with an *Ageing Population*

1) <u>Encouraging larger families</u>, e.g. in Italy women are offered <u>cash rewards</u> to have more children. This <u>increases</u> the <u>number of young people</u> — when they start work there will be a <u>larger working population</u> to pay taxes and support the ageing population.

2) <u>Encouraging</u> the <u>immigration</u> of <u>young people</u> from other countries. This <u>increases</u> the <u>working population</u> so there are <u>more people</u> paying taxes to support the ageing population.

> These strategies <u>don't help</u> towards <u>sustainable development</u> because they <u>increase</u> the <u>population size</u>.

3) <u>Raising</u> the <u>retirement age</u> — people <u>stay in work longer</u> and contribute to state pensions and personal pensions for <u>longer</u>. They will also <u>claim</u> the <u>state pension</u> for <u>less time</u>.

4) <u>Raising taxes</u> for the working population — this would <u>increase</u> the amount of <u>money available</u> to support the ageing population.

> These strategies <u>help</u> towards <u>sustainable development</u> because they help to <u>reduce the impacts</u> of an ageing population, <u>without increasing</u> the <u>population size</u>.

What are taxes, Grandpa?

You'll see, Jimmy. You'll see...

Being old is not a crime but my great-aunt has knitted some criminal jumpers...

'Live long enough to be a burden on your children' — I thought it was just a phrase... Learn about the <u>social</u> and <u>economic impacts</u> an ageing population can have, and the <u>strategies</u> governments have come up with to deal with them.

Ageing Populations — Case Study

Like lots of MEDCs around the world, the UK has an ageing population. This case study's got lots of juicy statistics you can use in your exam answers, so get swotting.

The UK's Population is Ageing

In 2005, 16% of the population of the UK was over 65. By 2041 this could be 25%.

The Ageing Population is Caused by Increasing Life Expectancy and Dropping Birth Rate

1) People are living longer because of advances in medicine and improved living standards. Between 1980 and 2006 life expectancy rose 2.6 years for women and 6.4 years for men — it's currently 81.5 for women and 77.2 for men. This means the proportion of older people in the population is going up.

2) Lots of babies were born in the 1940s and 1960s — periods called 'baby booms'. Those born in the 1940s are retiring now, creating a 'pensioner boom'.

3) Since the 1970s, the number of babies born has fallen. With fewer young people in the population the proportion of older people goes up.

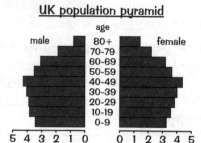
UK population pyramid
male / female
age: 80+, 70-79, 60-69, 50-59, 40-49, 30-39, 20-29, 10-19, 0-9
5 4 3 2 1 0   0 1 2 3 4 5
numbers / millions

The UK's Ageing Population Causes a few Problems

1) More elderly people are living in poverty — the working population isn't large enough to pay for a decent pension, and many people don't have other savings.

2) Even though the state pension is low the government is struggling to pay it. The taxes paid by people in work aren't enough to cover the cost of pensions and as the population ages the situation is getting worse.

3) The health service is under pressure because older people need more medical care than younger people. For example, in 2005 the average stay in hospital for people over 75 was 13 nights, but for the whole of the UK the average stay was only 8 nights.

There are Strategies to Influence Population Change in the UK

1) Encourage women to have children — working family tax credits support women (and men) who go back to work after their children are born. This makes it more affordable for couples to have children.

2) Encourage immigration of young people to the UK — the UK has allowed immigration of people from countries that joined the EU in 2004. Around 80% of immigrants from new EU countries in 2004 were 34 or under. This increases the number of people paying taxes, which helps to pay for the state pension and services.

There are other Strategies to Cope with the Problems of an Ageing Population

1) Raise the retirement age — the retirement age in the UK is currently 65 for men and 60 for women. This is going to change in stages, so that by 2046 it will be 68 for everyone. People will have to work for longer, so there will be more people paying tax and fewer claiming a pension.

2) Encourage people to take out private pensions — the government gives tax breaks for some types of private pension. With private pensions, people won't be so dependent on the state pension.

The strategies that influence population change increase the population. So they don't help towards sustainable development as more resources are used. The strategies to cope with the problems are more sustainable as they don't increase the population.

The Blurb
STATE PENSION AGE RAISED TO 105

Ageing population impact — sales of toilet roll covers are through the roof...

This case study is perfect exam fodder. Nothing makes an examiner's eyes spin like fruit machines more than real-life examples. Memorise the facts and figures from this page and you'll be all set up to get top marks in your exam.

Migration

Migration is the movement of people from one area to another area. Alas, they don't just do it for the fun of it — you need to learn the reasons why, as well as some good ol' impacts.

People Migrate Within Countries and To Different Countries

1) When people move into an area, it's called immigration. The people are called immigrants.

2) When people exit an area, it's called emigration. The people are called emigrants.

3) People can move to different countries — this is known as international migration. It might be across the world, or just a few miles over a border.

4) People can move between different regions within countries, e.g. from the countryside to a city (called rural-urban migration). This is known as internal migration.

There are two main types of migrant:

Refugees are people who've been forced to leave their country due to things like war, persecution or a natural disaster, e.g. thousands of refugees migrated to escape the war in Kosovo in 1999.

Economic migrants are people who move voluntarily from poorer places to richer places looking for jobs or higher wages, e.g. from Mexico to the USA. They often migrate so they can earn more money and then send some back to family in their country of origin.

Migration Happens Because of Push and Pull Factors

The reasons a person migrates can be classified as either push or pull factors:

Push factors are negative things about a person's place of origin (where they originally lived) that make them want to leave.

Pull factors are positive things about a person's destination that attract them to the destination.

EXAMPLE PUSH FACTORS:

Economic:
- A shortage of jobs.
- Low wages.

Social:
- Poor standard of living.
- Poor healthcare and education.

Political:
- Being persecuted because of religion or political views.
- War.

Environmental:
- Natural disasters like earthquakes or floods.
- A poor environment due to pollution or crime.

EXAMPLE PULL FACTORS:

Economic:
- More employment opportunities.
- Higher wages.

Social:
- Better standard of living.
- Better healthcare and education.

Political:
- Being free to worship as they like or join any political party.
- No war.

Environmental:
- A safe place with little crime or risk of natural disasters.
- A cleaner environment.

Umm-igration is when you don't know whether you're coming or going...

Migration sounds like a rough business, people being pushed and pulled all over the place. Remember, push factors are bad things about the place of origin that push people out, and pull factors are good things about the destination that pull them in.

Impacts of International Migration

International migration causes population change in a country, which leads to problems for both countries involved — the country that's been left behind (country of origin) and the country that people are moving to (the destination country). I always feel sorry for the country of origin — no one likes being left behind.

International Migration has Positive and Negative Impacts

International migration has impacts on the country of origin:

POSITIVE IMPACTS:
- There's less pressure on services like hospitals and schools, as there are fewer people.
- Money is usually sent back to the country of origin by emigrants.

NEGATIVE IMPACTS:
- Labour shortage — it's mostly people of working age that emigrate.
- Skills shortage — it tends to be the most skilled and educated people who emigrate.
- There's a high proportion of older people left, who can't work and often need care.

International migration also has impacts on the destination country:

POSITIVE IMPACTS:
- There's a bigger labour force in the destination country as young people immigrate to find work.
- Migrant workers pay taxes that help to fund services.

NEGATIVE IMPACTS:
- Locals and immigrants compete for jobs, which can cause tension and conflict.
- The increased demand for services can lead to overcrowding in hospitals and schools.
- Some of the money earned by immigrants is sent home rather than spent in the destination country.

There are Different Ways to Manage International Migration

Different countries manage international migration in different ways. Here are a few examples:

POINTS-BASED SYSTEMS

Points-based systems let countries choose who they want to let in. People who want to move are given points for things like age, education, work experience and whether they speak the language. Only those with enough points are allowed in, so in theory only the most skilled immigrants who'll adapt well are allowed to enter. Australia, New Zealand and Canada use systems like this.

LIMITS AND TARGETS

Limits and targets are set by some countries to make sure they don't let in too many or too few immigrants (although having too few is less likely to be a problem for most countries). The limits are set by looking at things like how many jobs are available and public opinion. If the limit has already been reached that year, no one else is allowed in.

6.1

8.5

BORDER CONTROL

CONTROLLING ILLEGAL IMMIGRATION

Lots of countries, especially MEDCs, have problems with people entering illegally or staying after they should have left (e.g. at the end of a holiday). In many countries illegal immigrants can be arrested and forced to leave the country. Italy fines and deports illegal immigrants, and people can go to jail for knowingly housing an illegal immigrant.

Another positive impact — yummy Polish sausage being sold in Tesco....

Immigration is a tricky issue. Politicians love arguing about it and examiners love quizzing you about it — so you really need to understand it. It has its downsides but there are benefits too, like more taxes being paid, yay.

International Migration — Case Study

There's been lots of <u>economic migration</u> from <u>Poland</u> to the <u>UK</u> in recent years — must be for the weather.

There are Economic Migrations to the UK

More than <u>half a million</u> people from Poland came <u>to the UK</u> between <u>2004</u> and <u>2007</u>.
The big move was <u>caused</u> by <u>push and pull factors</u>:

<u>PUSH factors</u> from Poland:

1) <u>High unemployment</u> — around <u>19%</u>.

2) <u>Low average wages</u> — about <u>one third</u> of the average EU wage.

3) <u>Housing shortages</u> — just over <u>300</u> dwellings for every <u>1000 people</u>.

<u>PULL factors</u> to the UK:

1) <u>Ease of migration</u> — the UK <u>allowed unlimited migration</u> from the EU in 2004 (it was <u>restricted</u> in some EU countries).

2) <u>More work and higher wages</u> — wages in the UK were <u>higher</u> and there was a <u>big demand</u> for <u>tradesmen</u>, e.g. plumbers.

3) <u>Good exchange rate</u> — the <u>pound</u> was <u>worth a lot</u> of <u>Polish currency</u>, so sending a few pounds back to Poland made a <u>big difference</u> to family at home.

All the moving around has <u>consequences</u> for both Poland and the UK:

IMPACTS IN POLAND

1) <u>Economic</u> — there was a <u>shortage of workers</u> in Poland, <u>slowing</u> the <u>growth</u> of the <u>economy</u>. But the Polish <u>economy</u> was <u>boosted</u> by the money <u>sent home</u> from emigrants — around €3 billion was sent to Poland from abroad in 2006.

2) <u>Social</u> — <u>most</u> of the people who <u>left</u> Poland were <u>young</u>. This led to an <u>ageing</u> population. But the young people who left <u>didn't need houses</u> or <u>jobs any more</u>, which <u>helped</u> with the <u>housing shortages</u> and <u>unemployment problems</u>.

IMPACTS IN THE UK

1) <u>Economic</u> — immigration <u>boosted</u> the UK <u>economy</u>, but a lot of the money earned in the UK was <u>sent back to Poland</u>. <u>New shops</u> selling Polish products <u>opened</u> to serve new Polish communities. Polish workers <u>pay taxes</u> that help <u>support</u> the UK's older <u>retired people</u>.

2) <u>Social</u> — some people in the UK were <u>unhappy</u> about the large numbers of Polish immigrants.

3) <u>Political</u> — politicians <u>changed the policy</u> on allowing <u>unlimited people</u> from new EU member states to immigrate because some people were unhappy about the immigrants (see below).

There are also <u>environmental impacts</u> — increased immigration has meant <u>more air traffic</u> between Poland and the UK. This has meant <u>more greenhouse gases</u> being released, <u>worsening global warming</u>.

The UK has now Changed How it Manages Immigration

1) Immigrants from Poland entering the UK <u>aren't limited</u> in number, but they do have to <u>register</u> under the <u>Worker Registration Scheme</u> if they want to work in the UK.

2) This lets the <u>UK Border Agency</u> <u>monitor how many</u> people are coming into the country, what <u>type</u> of <u>work</u> they're doing and the <u>effect</u> this is having on the UK <u>economy</u>.

3) The <u>large number</u> of Polish immigrants <u>entering</u> the UK led to some <u>complaints</u> — some people thought the resources in the UK wouldn't be able to <u>cope</u> with all the new people, e.g. there <u>wouldn't</u> be <u>enough jobs</u> or <u>housing</u> to go around.

4) In response to this, the Government <u>tightened</u> the <u>control</u> of migration from some of the <u>newer EU</u> states. For example, immigrants from the two newest EU states, <u>Bulgaria</u> and <u>Romania</u>, have to <u>get permission</u> from the <u>Home Office</u> to work in the UK (and this is only granted for <u>certain types</u> of jobs).

Economic migration — the money's getting away...

Funnily enough, lots of people really <u>want</u> to come and live in the <u>UK</u>. Sure Australia's got better weather and the trains in Italy always run on time, but we've got the Queen, weak tea and the jewel in the crown... Blackpool.

Revision Summary for Section Three

That's another smashing section under your belt — congratulations, oh studious one. And here's a delightful array of questions so you can check you've taken it all in. If you'd care to begin...

1) a) Under what circumstances does natural increase happen to a population?

   b) Under what circumstances does natural decrease happen to a population?

2) What happens to death rate at Stage 2 of the DTM?

3) What happens to birth rate at Stage 3 of the DTM?

4) Are LEDCs or MEDCs more likely to be in the early stages of the DTM?

5) What is the population structure of a country?

6) What do population pyramids show?

7) Give one reason why birth rate is high during Stage 1 of the DTM.

8) Describe how changes in agriculture affect the population growth rate.

9) Give one reason why the birth rate falls rapidly during Stage 3 of the DTM.

10) Briefly describe the population structure of a country in Stage 5 of the DTM.

11) Give two social impacts and two environmental impacts of overpopulation.

12) Give one economic impact of a youthful population.

13) Give an example of a strategy a country could use to control overpopulation.

14) Describe what it means for a country to develop in a way that's sustainable.

15) For a case study you know:

   a) Describe a policy used to try to control overpopulation.

   b) Give one piece of evidence that shows how effective this policy has been.

16) What is an ageing population?

17) What causes an ageing population?

18) Give one economic impact and one social impact of an ageing population.

19) Describe one strategy to cope with an ageing population.

20) a) Name a country that has an ageing population and describe what caused it.

   b) For the country you've named, describe one problem caused by the ageing population.

   c) Give one strategy used by the country to influence population change.
      Explain how it helps, and comment on its sustainability.

21) Define 'migration'.

22) What's it called when a person moves into an area?

23) a) Explain what 'push factors' and 'pull factors' are in migration.

   b) Give an example of a pull factor.

24) Give one negative impact of migration on the country of origin.

25) Give one positive impact of migration on the destination country.

26) Describe one way in which international migration can be managed.

27) a) Give one push factor and one pull factor to explain why people have emigrated
      to a country you have studied.

   b) Give one impact of this migration on the country of origin and one on the destination country.

   c) Describe a strategy the destination country uses to try to control international migration.

Urbanisation

Urban areas (towns and cities) are the place to be... or so I'm told by my mate who tucks his tracksuit bottoms into his socks. People are upping sticks and moving to cities, and you've got to know all about it.

Urbanisation is Happening Fastest in LEDCs

Urbanisation is the growth in the proportion of a country's population living in urban areas. It's happening in countries all over the world — more than 50% of the world's population currently live in urban areas (3.4 billion people) and this is increasing every day. But urbanisation differs between MEDCs and LEDCs:

1) Most of the population in MEDCs already live in urban areas, e.g. more than 80% of the UK's population live in urban areas.

2) Not many of the population in LEDCs currently live in urban areas, e.g. around 25% of the population of Bangladesh live in urban areas.

3) Most urbanisation that's happening in the world today is going on in LEDCs and it's happening at a fast pace.

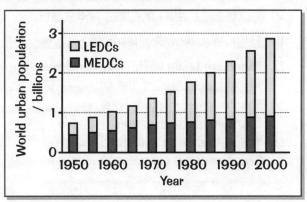

Urbanisation is Caused by Rural-urban Migration...

Rural-urban migration is the movement of people from the countryside to the cities. The reasons people want to leave the countryside are called PUSH factors. They include:

1) Few jobs and low wages — mechanisation of farming is leading to the loss of jobs in rural areas. Also the jobs that are available are often low paid, which can lead to poverty.

2) Lack of services — there's often no access to services or very poor services in rural areas, e.g. few shops, schools and health centres.

3) Poor harvests — in rural areas in LEDCs some people are subsistence farmers. This means they grow food to feed their family and sell any extra to make a small income. Poor harvests and crop failures can mean they make no income and even risk starvation.

The reasons people want to move to urban areas are called PULL factors. They include:

1) More jobs and higher wages — there are more jobs available in cities and they pay more. Also, the jobs offer a more stable income compared to other jobs, e.g. in farming. Industry is attracted to cities because there's a larger workforce and better infrastructure (e.g. roads) than in rural areas.

2) Better services — there's better access to services like healthcare in cities. Also, there's greater access to things like clean water and electricity.

...And Good Healthcare and a High Birth Rate in Cities

It's normally young people who move to cities to find work. These people have children in the cities, which increases the proportion of the population living in urban areas. Also, better healthcare in urban areas means people live longer, again increasing the proportion of people in urban areas.

Dick Whittington and His Cat — the classic rural-urban migration case study...

So the push factors are the bad things about rural areas like the constant smell of manure and tractor-related traffic jams. The pull factors are the good things about the cities like the joy of the tube at rush hour and 24-hour bars.

Impacts of Urbanisation

If you think your living room is too cramped, or your bathroom's just not big enough, then spare a thought for people who live where there's tonnes of <u>urbanisation</u> — it can get <u>massively overcrowded</u>.

Urbanisation has Many Impacts

Urbanisation causes problems in both the <u>urban areas</u> that people move to and the <u>rural areas</u> they leave:

The impacts of <u>urbanisation</u> in <u>urban areas</u> include:

1) <u>Overcrowding</u> — <u>too many people</u> leads to a <u>shortage</u> of <u>houses and jobs</u>.

2) <u>Increased traffic</u>, <u>pollution</u> and <u>waste</u>.

In <u>LEDCs</u>, overcrowding leads to <u>squatter settlements</u>:

1) These are <u>badly built</u>, <u>illegal</u> settlements found <u>in and around</u> the city. ⟹

2) They're <u>overcrowded</u>, so <u>disease spreads quickly</u>. There are <u>no drains</u>, so <u>flooding</u> is <u>common</u>.

3) They often <u>don't</u> have <u>basic services</u> like <u>electricity</u>, <u>sewers</u> or <u>firefighters</u>.

Squatter settlements are also called shanty towns.

No electricity or phone lines

Houses built from waste material like plastic sheets

Little space between houses

No paved roads or sewers

There are squatter settlements in São Paulo (Brazil) and Mumbai (India).

©iStockphoto.com/Nitin Sanil

In <u>rural areas</u>, the <u>population falls</u> as people move to the cities. This leads to problems:

1) An <u>increasingly elderly population</u> — <u>young people move</u> away, <u>leaving older people behind</u>. They may then <u>struggle</u> with <u>tasks like shopping</u>, which young relatives helped them with.

2) <u>Even fewer services</u> — <u>less demand</u> due to the falling population means some <u>shops and services close</u>. Also, there are <u>fewer taxes</u> being collected to pay for services, so some may close due to a <u>lack of funding</u>.

Governments try to Manage the Impacts of Urbanisation

The <u>impacts</u> in <u>urban areas</u> are managed by improving the problems caused by <u>too many people</u>. For example:

1) <u>Building more houses</u> and <u>attracting more industry</u> to create <u>more jobs</u>.

2) <u>Easing traffic</u> and <u>pollution</u> by <u>improving public transport</u> and <u>roads</u>, and <u>promoting cycling</u>.

3) <u>Improving services</u> like <u>water</u> and <u>electricity</u>.

4) In LEDCs, governments can try to <u>improve squatter settlements</u>. For example:

- <u>Self-help schemes</u> — the government <u>supplies materials</u> so people can <u>build their own homes</u>.

- <u>Site and service schemes</u> — people <u>pay</u> a <u>low rent</u> for a site and the money is used to <u>provide basic services</u> for the area.

The <u>problems</u> of <u>urbanisation</u> in <u>rural areas</u> can be managed by <u>easing the push factors</u>, so people <u>don't move away</u>. For example:

1) <u>Investing in local services</u> like healthcare — this will <u>provide jobs</u> and <u>encourage</u> more people to <u>stay</u>.

2) <u>Giving loans</u> and <u>grants to businesses</u> if they <u>move there</u> — this <u>encourages companies</u> to <u>set up</u> in <u>rural areas</u>, which <u>creates jobs</u>.

3) <u>Improving local transport</u> — good public transport will make <u>travelling</u> around <u>easier for local people</u>. People could <u>still travel to the city</u> for <u>work</u> but stay <u>living</u> in the rural areas.

BETTER BUS LTD.

Some residents try to win 'Who Wants to Be a Millionaire'...

<u>Urbanisation</u> causes a lot of <u>problems</u> for everyone. It's enough to make you wonder <u>why</u> people bother moving in the first place... the <u>push</u> and <u>pull factors</u>, of course. My memory really is a sieve — we only covered them <u>one page ago</u>.

Urbanisation — Case Study

China's population is 1.3 billion. That's 21 times as many as the UK or 400 million times as many as my house.

Push and Pull Factors have Caused Urbanisation in China

Urbanisation in China is being caused by the internal migration of people from rural areas to urban areas (rural-urban migration). In 1990 around 26% of the population lived in urban areas, but by 2006 a whopping 44% did (over 550 million people). Urbanisation is happening because of push and pull factors.

PUSH factors from rural areas:

1) Fewer jobs — more machinery has made farming more efficient, so fewer workers are needed. This has created high unemployment, e.g. 150 million rural people were unemployed in 2004.

2) Lower wages and higher poverty — wages are normally lower in rural areas in China, leading to more poverty. E.g. in 2004 there were 26.1 million people in rural areas in poverty.

3) Shortage of services — services like education and healthcare are funded by taxes collected within the local area. This means poor rural areas don't have the money to improve their services.

PULL factors to urban areas:

1) More jobs — there are more industries and jobs in urban areas.

2) Higher wages and lower poverty — the average income is three times higher in urban areas than in rural areas.

3) Better services — there are more (and better) education and healthcare services in urban areas because there's more money to pay for them. For example, lack of funding in rural areas meant that in 2002, 1.1 million children couldn't go to primary school.

Urbanisation in China has had Lots of Impacts

There are impacts of urbanisation in the urban areas, e.g. Beijing:

1) Positive — more workers and an increase in the demand for services in the urban areas helps to increase trade and industry. This is good for the economy.

2) Negative — the increasing population causes more pollution and environmental damage. Over 270 cities in China have no water treatment plants so sewage is dumped straight into local rivers.

And yes, there are impacts for the rural areas too:

1) Positive — about 130 million people who've left rural areas to work in towns send money home to their families. This increases their income and helps them to avoid poverty.

2) Negative — it's usually the young people who migrate, leaving an ageing population behind. About half of all Chinese people aged over 60 now live without any younger relatives to help look after them.

Urbanisation is Being Managed in China

China is trying to manage the problems of urbanisation in both rural and urban areas. For example:

1) Urban — in 2001, China changed its water supply system so it could cope with the increased sewage and pollution in urban areas. This helped to improve both water quality and supply.

2) Rural — in 2009, a pilot pension scheme was set up to give retired farmers a pension every month. This will help to raise income and reduce poverty in rural areas.

Excitement was in the air over the 2008 Olympics, and also lead and benzene...

Sounds like there's an awful lot of people rushing around China — that's one stampede I wouldn't want to get caught in. I can't cope with the stampede in the shopping centre at sales time. Just the thought makes me want to lie down.

Counter-urbanisation

Woah there, now this does sound like an <u>exciting topic</u>. It's a wonder these <u>geographers sleep</u> at night.

Counter-urbanisation is Happening in MEDCs

<u>Counter-urbanisation</u> is the <u>opposite</u> of <u>urbanisation</u> — it's people moving <u>out of cities</u> and <u>into rural areas</u>. It's happening <u>more</u> in <u>MEDCs</u> and here's <u>why</u>:

Counter-urbanisation is also called deurbanisation.

PUSH factors

1) <u>Pollution</u> and <u>traffic congestion</u> are <u>higher</u> in cities.
2) <u>Crime rates</u> are also often <u>higher</u>.
3) <u>Houses</u> in cities can <u>cost more</u>.

PULL factors

1) <u>Better transport links</u> and <u>increased car ownership</u> mean people can easily <u>commute</u> to work in cities.
2) The <u>growth of IT</u> (e.g. e-mail, internet) means more people can <u>work from home</u>.
3) <u>New out-of-town business parks</u> mean <u>more jobs</u> are available <u>outside cities</u>.

Counter-urbanisation has... You Guessed it... Lots of Impacts

Sale £10 million

<u>Rural impacts:</u>

1) <u>Increased demand</u> for houses <u>drives up house prices</u>. Young people <u>can't afford</u> to buy homes, so have to <u>move away</u>, which can lead to resentment.
2) Many <u>commuters prefer</u> to use <u>shops</u> and <u>services closer to work</u>. This means <u>local ones</u> may <u>shut down</u> due to <u>lack of demand</u>. As a result, local people who <u>don't</u> have <u>transport</u> have <u>no access</u> to <u>services</u> and become <u>isolated</u>.
3) People <u>leave commuter villages</u> (villages where most people commute to the city) during the <u>day</u>, so the village is largely <u>empty</u> then. This can cause a <u>decline</u> in <u>community spirit</u>.

<u>Urban impacts:</u>

1) <u>Inner city areas</u> with high <u>crime</u> and <u>pollution</u> become <u>more empty</u> and <u>disused</u> as people move away. This makes them <u>more unpopular</u>, so they get more and more <u>run-down</u>.
2) <u>Commuters</u> prefer to shop and work on the <u>outskirts</u> of the city. So <u>services</u> and <u>shops</u> in the <u>centre</u> <u>lose customers</u> and <u>close</u>.

Governments try to Manage the Impacts of Counter-urbanisation

<u>Governments</u> try to <u>manage</u> the problems caused by counter-urbanisation in...

...<u>rural areas</u> by:

1) Making <u>policies</u> to provide <u>more housing</u> for <u>local people</u> — these can <u>stop</u> <u>commuters</u> and <u>second home buyers</u> from getting houses. E.g. in the <u>Yorkshire Dales</u>, <u>new housing</u> is <u>only</u> <u>available</u> for people who <u>work locally</u>.
2) <u>Investing in services</u> — governments can provide <u>extra money</u> for <u>services</u> in <u>commuter villages</u>, so they <u>don't</u> <u>close down</u>.

...<u>urban areas</u> by:

1) <u>Redeveloping urban areas</u> — this makes them <u>more attractive</u> places, which <u>slows down counter-urbanisation</u> and encourages people to <u>move back</u>, e.g. the <u>Albert Dock</u> <u>development</u> <u>in Liverpool</u>.

   When people move back into cities it's called re-urbanisation.

2) <u>Regenerating shopping areas</u>, e.g. by <u>pedestrianising</u> them (stopping car access), having <u>better public transport links</u> and <u>better car parking</u>. This makes them <u>more attractive</u>.

Right, that's it, everybody just STAY WHERE YOU ARE...

That's the trouble with <u>society today</u> — everyone's scurrying about, from <u>town</u> to <u>country</u> and <u>back again</u>, thinking the grass will be greener in the next place. Now if you'll excuse me, the removal van is here and I still have boxes to pack.

Urban Land Use

Every city is different, but they all have <u>dodgy run-down parts</u> and <u>posh housing areas</u>. Obviously you should use more <u>formal terms</u> to describe them in the exam — amazingly enough, they're all listed below...

A City can be Split into Four Main Parts

Cities are usually made up of <u>four parts</u> — each part has a <u>different land use</u> (e.g. housing or industrial).
The land use of each part <u>stays fairly similar</u> from <u>city to city</u>, but it <u>can differ</u> a bit (see below).
The diagram below is a <u>view from above</u> of a <u>typical city</u> — it shows <u>roughly</u> where the four parts are:

CBD
This is the <u>central business district</u>.
It's usually found right in the <u>centre</u>
of a city. It's the <u>commercial centre</u>
of the city with <u>shops</u> and <u>offices</u>.

The inner city
This part is found <u>around the CBD</u>. It has a
mix of <u>poorer quality housing</u> (like high-rise
tower blocks) and <u>older industrial buildings</u>.

This is just a model
— no city looks
exactly like this.

The suburbs
These are <u>housing areas</u> found
<u>towards the edge</u> of the city.

The rural-urban fringe
This is the part <u>right at the edge</u> of
a city, where there are <u>both urban
land uses</u> (e.g. factories) and
<u>rural land uses</u> (e.g. farming).

Land Use is decided by Social, Economic and Cultural Factors

Part of city	Land use	Social factors	Economic factors	Cultural factors
CBD	<u>Businesses</u>, e.g. <u>shops</u> and <u>offices</u>	It's <u>busy</u> and very <u>accessible</u>.	Land is <u>expensive</u> (only businesses can afford it).	It's a centre point for <u>entertainment</u>, e.g. <u>cinemas</u>.
Inner city	<u>Low-class housing</u> and <u>industry</u>	Traditionally <u>small houses</u> were built here <u>near to factories</u> to <u>house workers</u>.	<u>Poorer people</u> who <u>can't afford</u> to <u>commute</u> and can only afford <u>small houses</u> live here.	<u>Ethnic groups</u> live here so they're <u>near</u> to <u>important services</u>, e.g. places of worship.
Suburbs	<u>Medium-class housing</u>	It's <u>less crowded</u> and <u>more pleasant</u>, with <u>less traffic</u> and <u>pollution</u>.	<u>Richer people</u> who <u>can afford</u> to <u>commute</u> and to have <u>big houses</u> live here.	People with <u>families</u> live here due to the <u>space</u> for <u>leisure activities</u>, e.g. BBQs.
Rural-urban fringe	<u>Business parks</u> and <u>high-class housing</u>	It's <u>still accessible</u> for <u>commuters</u> and there's <u>lots</u> of <u>space</u>.	The <u>land</u> is often <u>cheaper</u> here so <u>bigger houses</u> can be built for <u>richer people</u>.	<u>Richer people</u> who like a <u>rural lifestyle</u> and being in <u>reach of the city</u> live here.

The Land Use of the Parts can Differ from City to City

1) Sometimes the <u>land use</u> of each part <u>doesn't match the model</u> above — real cities are all
   <u>slightly different</u>. For example, in <u>LEDC cities</u> like Rio de Janeiro, there's usually <u>low-cost housing</u>
   and <u>squatter settlements</u> on the <u>outskirts</u> of cities, but <u>high-class housing</u> in the <u>CBD</u>.

2) The <u>land use</u> of each part of a city can also <u>change over time</u>, for example:
   - In recent years a lot of <u>shopping centres</u> have been built in <u>out-of-town</u> locations in the UK,
     e.g. Meadowhall Shopping Centre was built on the outskirts of Sheffield in 1990.
   - <u>Inner city tower blocks</u> have been <u>removed</u> and <u>replaced</u> with <u>housing estates</u>
     on the <u>rural-urban fringe</u>, e.g. this has happened in Birmingham.

Just popping into the rural-urban fringe to do a bit of shopping...

You need to know about the <u>four main parts</u> of a city and the <u>land use</u> in each bit, but remember that the land use <u>isn't</u> <u>the same everywhere</u> — I'm sure city planners do this on purpose, just to make your revision awkward. Some people...

Urban Development

Urbanisation has led to <u>overcrowding</u> in my house — I have to <u>share a room</u> with my brother. Something must be done I tell you. Maybe a small development over the garage to house him.

Planners <u>Look at Social, Economic and Environmental</u> Needs

<u>Planners</u> need to look at the <u>social</u>, <u>economic</u> and <u>environmental</u> needs of the <u>population</u> when <u>designing new developments</u>. For example:

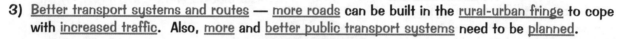

These inner city golf courses may be small but at least my handicap is amazing.

Social needs

1) <u>More housing</u> — this can be built on old <u>industrial sites</u> (<u>brownfield sites</u>) near the <u>city centre</u>, or on the <u>rural-urban fringe</u> for <u>commuters</u>.

2) <u>More room for social activities</u> — e.g. <u>parks</u> replace <u>brownfield sites</u> in cities and places for activities like <u>golf</u> are set up in the <u>rural-urban fringe</u>.

3) <u>Better transport systems and routes</u> — <u>more roads</u> can be built in the <u>rural-urban fringe</u> to cope with <u>increased traffic</u>. Also, <u>more</u> and <u>better public transport systems</u> need to be <u>planned</u>.

Economic needs

<u>More jobs</u> — <u>business parks</u> and <u>out-of-town shopping centres</u> can be built on <u>undeveloped land</u> (<u>greenfield sites</u>) in the <u>rural-urban fringe</u> where land is <u>cheap</u> and it's <u>easily accessible</u>.

Environmental needs

1) <u>More waste disposal systems</u> — <u>landfill sites</u> can be built on the <u>rural-urban fringe</u> to cope with the <u>increase</u> in <u>waste</u>.

2) <u>More green spaces</u> — <u>derelict land</u> in cities can be turned back into open spaces.

<u>Some Developments</u> are More Sustainable than Others

<u>Sustainable</u> means doing things in a way that lets the people <u>living now</u> have the things they need, but <u>without stopping</u> people in the <u>future</u> <u>meeting their needs</u>. Basically, it means <u>not irreversibly damaging the environment</u> or <u>using up resources</u> faster than they can be replaced. Some urban <u>developments</u> are <u>more sustainable</u> than others. For example:

Carbon-neutral homes

<u>Carbon-neutral homes</u> are buildings that <u>generate</u> as much <u>energy</u> as they <u>use</u>, e.g. by using <u>solar panels</u> to <u>produce energy</u>. For example, <u>BedZED</u> is a carbon-neutral housing development in London. <u>More homes</u> can be provided without <u>damaging the environment</u> too much or causing <u>much more pollution</u>. These are <u>more sustainable</u> than bog-standard houses.

Building on brownfield sites

Using brownfield sites for <u>new buildings</u> <u>stops green space being used up</u>. So the <u>space</u> will <u>still be available</u> for people in the <u>future</u>. This is <u>more sustainable</u> than building on <u>greenfield sites</u> (sites that <u>haven't been built on before</u>). For example, the <u>London Docklands</u> redevelopment was built on a brownfield site.

More efficient public transport systems

<u>Good public transport systems</u> encourage <u>less car use</u>, which <u>reduces pollution</u> and <u>traffic</u>. Also, more <u>efficient vehicles</u> that <u>use less fuel</u> use <u>fewer resources</u> and give out <u>less pollution</u>. E.g. some buses in <u>London</u> are powered by <u>hydrogen</u> and only emit <u>water vapour</u>.

Include recycling facilities in developments

<u>More recycling</u> means <u>fewer resources</u> are used, e.g. metal cans can be used to make <u>more</u> cans. Also, <u>less waste</u> is produced, which reduces the amount that goes to <u>landfill</u>. Landfill is <u>unsustainable</u> as it <u>wastes resources</u> and <u>eventually</u> there'll be <u>nowhere left</u> to <u>bury the waste</u>.

<u>Conserve water resources — if it's brown, flush it down, if it's yellow, let it mellow...</u>

<u>Sustainability's</u> a tough one to get your head around. Make sure you're clear on <u>what it means</u> before you memorise <u>all the ways developments</u> can be made <u>more sustainable</u>. Then you can think about sustaining yourself with a brew.

Urban Development — Case Study

The <u>best thing</u> about <u>geography</u> is the many exotic <u>case studies</u>. This case study will introduce you to an exotic land far, far away. Or at least a little bit away. Yes, it's Glasgow, Scotland.

Glasgow is being Developed

<u>Glasgow</u> is the largest city in Scotland, with a <u>population</u> of over <u>580 000 people</u>. The decline in <u>traditional industries</u>, such as <u>shipbuilding</u>, has led to changes to Glasgow's <u>social</u>, <u>economic</u> and <u>environmental</u> needs. For example:

1) Some areas of Glasgow, such as the <u>Gorbals</u>, have <u>poor quality</u>, <u>high-rise housing</u> that was built in the 1960s and <u>needs replacing</u>.

2) <u>More jobs</u> are needed as there's <u>high unemployment</u> in Glasgow. In 2008, <u>7.1%</u> of working age people in Glasgow were <u>unemployed</u>, compared to <u>4.9%</u> for the whole of <u>Scotland</u>.

But recently the city has been <u>benefiting</u> from major <u>redevelopments</u>:

Clyde Waterfront Regeneration Project

This project is helping to change <u>old inner city industrial</u> land, e.g. land that had <u>shipbuilding</u> yards on it. The land will now be used for <u>business</u>, <u>recreational</u> and <u>residential</u> developments. Over <u>200 projects</u> costing over <u>£5 billion</u> are ongoing including the <u>Glasgow Science Centre</u>, <u>new offices</u>, <u>shops</u>, <u>parks</u>, a <u>walkway</u> alongside the river and <u>improved transport services</u> (e.g. new buses).

Glasgow Science Centre

©iStockphoto.com

Regeneration in the Gorbals

<u>£170 million</u> is being invested in this <u>declining</u> neighbourhood. There's an ongoing project to build a new 'urban village' with over <u>1500 new homes</u>, a <u>shopping centre</u>, a <u>library</u>, a <u>community centre</u> and a <u>good quality bus service</u>.

The Developments Aim to Meet the Needs of the Local Population

1) <u>Social needs</u> — the projects will <u>improve transport</u> and <u>leisure facilities</u>, and <u>provide new homes</u>.

2) <u>Economic needs</u> — new <u>businesses</u> are being <u>attracted into the area</u>, bringing <u>jobs</u>. E.g. over <u>50 000</u> new jobs are being created in the <u>Waterfront Project</u> through the new businesses and building work.

3) <u>Environmental needs</u> — the areas will be <u>more attractive</u> and have more <u>green spaces</u>. E.g. the <u>Waterfront Project</u> will have various <u>parks</u> and <u>natural areas</u>.

The Developments Have Tried to be Sustainable

<u>Clyde Waterfront Regeneration Project</u>

1) It has <u>bus links</u>, and <u>walking</u> and <u>cycling routes</u> to encourage <u>lower car use</u>. This means <u>less pollution</u> and <u>fewer greenhouse gases</u> will be emitted. Also, <u>less fossil fuel</u> will be used, which <u>saves resources</u> for future use.

2) The development is on <u>derelict</u>, <u>brownfield sites</u>, which <u>saves land</u>.

3) A lot of <u>material</u> from <u>old buildings</u> has been <u>reused</u>, so <u>fewer resources</u> have been used up.

Police box

The regeneration of the gerbils is complete.

<u>Regeneration projects in the Gorbals:</u>

The development projects use <u>derelict</u>, <u>brownfield sites</u> to create new <u>green spaces</u> such as <u>Gorbals Park</u>. This <u>reuses land</u> and <u>makes space</u> for future generations to use.

It's bonnie on the clyde now...

Hope you enjoyed that trip to the distant <u>North</u>. Maybe you could send a postcard next time. I do love a good postcard, me. I'll daydream about postcards while you cover the page and <u>jot down</u> the finer points of this <u>case study</u>.

Retail Services

And now for a page about <u>shopping</u> — you get to think about <u>retail therapy</u> and call it <u>revision</u>. Bargain.

You Need to Know These Terms

1) There are <u>two types</u> of <u>consumer goods</u> (things people buy):
   - <u>High order goods</u> — these are goods that are <u>only bought occasionally</u> and are usually <u>more expensive</u>, e.g. clothes, furniture and cars. They're also called <u>comparison</u> goods.
   - <u>Low order goods</u> — these are goods that are <u>bought frequently</u> and are usually quite <u>cheap</u>, e.g. milk, bread and newspapers. They're also called <u>convenience</u> goods.

2) <u>The threshold population</u> — the <u>minimum population</u> needed to <u>support</u> a shop. Shops that <u>sell high order goods</u> have a <u>high threshold population</u>.

3) <u>The sphere of influence</u> — the <u>area</u> that <u>people come from</u> to visit a shop or an area. Shops that <u>sell high order goods</u> have a <u>large sphere of influence</u> because people <u>will travel</u> a long way <u>occasionally</u> to <u>buy expensive items</u>. People <u>won't</u> <u>travel</u> a long way to buy things they <u>need regularly</u>, so shops that <u>sell low order goods</u> will have a <u>small sphere of influence</u>. The <u>distance</u> people will <u>travel</u> for a <u>particular good or service</u> is called its <u>range</u>.

> Go on... you know you want to...

Different Shopping Areas have Different Characteristics

You need to <u>know</u> the <u>characteristics</u> of retail services in <u>urban</u> and <u>rural</u> areas:

	SHOPPING AREA	LOCATION	GOODS SOLD	THRESHOLD POPULATION	SPHERE OF INFLUENCE
URBAN	<u>City centre</u>	<u>CBD</u>	<u>High order</u>, e.g. clothes and jewellery.	<u>High</u> — because they sell <u>high order</u> goods and the <u>rent</u> is <u>expensive</u>.	<u>Large</u> — they attract people from a <u>wide area</u>.
URBAN	<u>Out-of-town shopping centre</u>	<u>Rural-urban fringe</u>	<u>High order</u>, e.g. clothes and hardware.	<u>Medium</u> — they sell <u>high order</u> goods but the cost of <u>rent</u> is <u>lower</u>.	<u>Large</u> — they attract people from a <u>wide area</u>.
URBAN	<u>Shopping parades</u> (short rows of shops)	<u>Suburbs</u>	<u>High</u> and <u>low order</u>, e.g. newspapers and clothes.	<u>Medium</u> — they sell a <u>mixture</u> of goods and the cost of <u>rent</u> is <u>lower</u> than in the city centre.	<u>Medium</u> — they attract people from the <u>nearby area</u>.
URBAN	<u>Corner shops</u>	<u>Inner city</u>	<u>Low order</u>, e.g. newspapers and bread.	<u>Low</u> — because they sell goods that are <u>bought often</u> and <u>rent</u> is <u>cheap</u>.	<u>Small</u> — they only attract <u>local customers</u>.
RURAL	<u>Village shops</u>	<u>Villages</u>	<u>Low order</u>, e.g. newspapers and bread.	<u>Low</u> — because they sell goods that are <u>bought often</u> and <u>rent</u> is <u>cheap</u>.	<u>Small</u> — they only attract <u>local customers</u>.

> The <u>size of a settlement</u> will also affect what shops can locate there — the <u>bigger</u> a settlement is, the <u>greater</u> its population, so shops will have <u>more potential customers</u>. So the <u>larger</u> a settlement, the <u>more likely</u> it is to have shops selling <u>high order</u> goods.

Some Rural Shops Sell High Order Goods

<u>Shops in rural areas</u> sell mainly <u>low order goods</u> (see above), but some specialist shops that have a <u>large sphere of influence</u> can be found there. People are willing to travel far to buy specialist, rural goods, e.g. <u>caravans</u> or <u>walking equipment</u> (they have a <u>large range</u>).

Homework — go into town and buy yourself some shoes...

Alright, just kidding. Your homework is actually to go into town and buy <u>me</u> some shoes. I like five-inch heels with polka dots, size 11. Then when you come back, see <u>how much</u> of this page you remember. Good luck to you.

Changing Retail Services — Case Study

We all know <u>fashions</u> come and go — for example, <u>corner shops</u> are out and <u>out-of-town shopping centres</u> are in. If you're not sure you can keep up with it all, maybe this page will help you along.

Retail Services Change Over Time

There have been <u>major changes</u> in the way we shop in the UK in the last 100 years.
This is mainly due to <u>two factors</u>:

CHANGES TO TRANSPORT

<u>Car ownership</u> has <u>increased</u> so people can <u>travel further</u> for their shopping. This means there are <u>fewer</u>, <u>smaller convenience stores</u> in <u>rural</u> areas, but there are <u>more out-of-town shopping centres</u>. They're built out of town because land is <u>cheaper</u>, there's <u>more available</u> and it's <u>accessible</u> with <u>on-site parking</u>.

CHANGING MARKET FORCES

1) <u>Changing market forces</u> means changes in the <u>supply</u> and <u>demand</u> for goods and retail services.
2) <u>Supply</u> is how <u>easy</u> and <u>cheap</u> it is to <u>get products</u>.
3) <u>Demand</u> is <u>what products</u> people <u>want</u> and <u>how much</u> they are willing to <u>pay</u> for them.
4) Basically, people now want a <u>larger range</u> of goods at <u>cheaper prices</u>.
5) <u>Smaller</u>, <u>specialist shops</u> <u>can't meet</u> this <u>demand</u>, but <u>larger chain stores</u> and <u>supermarkets</u> <u>can</u> — they have <u>lots</u> of <u>different products</u> under one roof at <u>much cheaper prices</u>, so people shop there instead.

<u>Social habits</u> and <u>work patterns</u> have also changed — people have <u>less time to shop</u> for the things they really <u>need</u> (e.g. food) but <u>want more leisure shopping</u> time (e.g. to shop for <u>clothes</u>). This means it's <u>convenient</u> to use <u>supermarkets</u>, which stock all <u>different types</u> of food all together.

Retail Services have Changed in South Yorkshire

<u>South Yorkshire</u> has a mixture of <u>rural</u> and <u>urban</u> areas, e.g. <u>Sheffield</u> and part of the <u>Peak District</u>.
In recent years the <u>provision</u> of <u>retail services</u> in this area has <u>changed</u>:

1) In <u>1990</u>, a large <u>out-of-town shopping centre</u> called <u>Meadowhall</u> was built near <u>Sheffield</u>. The centre has <u>280 shops</u>, is <u>easily accessible</u> by car and has <u>12 000 free parking spaces</u>. Around <u>800 000 shoppers</u> visit the centre <u>every week</u>.

2) The <u>number</u> of <u>shops</u> in <u>Sheffield city centre</u> has <u>declined</u>. Some, such as <u>House of Fraser</u>, have <u>moved to Meadowhall</u> where the <u>rent</u> is <u>cheaper</u> and they can have <u>more space</u>. Some have <u>closed down</u>, possibly because shoppers are going to Meadowhall <u>instead</u>. Early estimates suggested a <u>15% trade loss</u> from the city centre <u>due to</u> the building of Meadowhall.

3) There are also <u>fewer shops</u> and <u>Post Offices</u>® in the surrounding <u>rural villages</u>, such as <u>Hope</u>. This is because <u>more</u> people <u>own cars</u> and <u>travel</u> to urban areas to do their shopping.

<u>Sheffield city centre</u> is now fighting back by <u>redeveloping</u> itself, <u>improving parking</u> and using a '<u>City Watch</u>' scheme to <u>reduce crime</u>. (It's reet nice — why not go and have a look for yourself.)

I love geography — it encourages you to revise shopping...

It's a funny thing — lots of people talk wistfully about the good old days when there were lots of <u>small shops</u> with <u>real quality</u> and <u>proper service</u>. But I've seen them snaffling the last few tins of luxury baked beans down at Asda.

Revision Summary for Section Four

Phew, there was an awful lot going on in that section. We've been from the city to the countryside and back again, with a massive shopping trip at the end and a few regeneration projects thrown in for good measure. It's almost time to put your feet up and relax with a cup of tea, but first you need to find out whether you've taken in all the details of your epic journey. These questions will let you check whether you've really been paying attention or if you've just been along for the shoes.

1) What is urbanisation?

2) How does the rate of urbanisation differ between MEDCs and LEDCs?

3) What is rural-urban migration?

4) Give two push factors and two pull factors that help explain why rural-urban migration happens.

5) Explain what a squatter settlement is.

6) List two consequences of urbanisation in rural areas.

7) Describe two ways in which governments try to manage the problems of urbanisation.

8) a) Give an example of a country you have studied where urbanisation is taking place.

   b) Give two push factors that cause urbanisation in that country.

   c) Give two pull factors that cause urbanisation in that country.

9) What is counter-urbanisation?

10) Give three impacts of counter-urbanisation in rural areas.

11) How do governments try to manage the impacts of counter-urbanisation?

12) Name the four main parts of a city.

13) Which of the four parts of the city is furthest from the centre?

14) Which part of a city mainly has medium-class housing?

15) Describe the social, economic and cultural factors that have led to business parks and high-class housing being built in the rural-urban fringe.

16) List one social, one economic and one environmental need the population of a growing city may have.

17) What does sustainable mean?

18) Describe two types of sustainable urban development.

19) a) Name a city you have studied that is undergoing development.

   b) Give one economic and one social aim of the development.

   c) Describe how sustainable the development project is.

20) What are low order goods?

21) What is the threshold population for a shop?

22) Describe the goods sold, threshold population, sphere of influence and accessibility for shops in the following areas:

   a) CBD,

   b) rural-urban fringe.

23) What are the two main factors that have changed the way we shop in the UK in the last 100 years?

24) Describe how retail services in a named area have changed and what effects this has had on the surrounding area.

Tectonic Hazards and Tectonic Plates

Welcome, geographer, to your fifth section — it's the one everyone looks forward to. It's a <u>hazardous</u> one though — <u>earthquakes</u> and <u>volcanoes</u> are on the agenda, so keep your arms and legs in at all times.

Tectonic Hazards are a Type of Natural Hazard

1) A natural hazard is a naturally occurring <u>event</u> that has the potential to <u>affect people's lives</u> or <u>property</u>, e.g. earthquakes, volcanic eruptions and tsunamis.

2) When natural hazards <u>do affect</u> people's lives or property they're called <u>natural disasters</u>.

3) <u>Earthquakes</u> and <u>volcanoes</u> are <u>tectonic hazards</u> — they're <u>caused</u> by the <u>movement of tectonic plates</u>.

The Earth's Surface is Separated into Tectonic Plates

1) At the <u>centre</u> of the Earth is the <u>core</u> — it has an inner bit and an outer bit. The <u>inner</u> core is a ball of <u>solid iron and nickel</u>. The <u>outer</u> core is <u>liquid</u>.

2) Around the core is the <u>mantle</u>, which is <u>semi-molten rock</u> that <u>moves very slowly</u>.

3) The <u>outer layer</u> of the Earth is the <u>crust</u>. It's very <u>thin</u> (about <u>20 km</u>).

4) The crust is <u>divided</u> into lots of slabs called <u>tectonic plates</u> (they float on the mantle). Plates are made of <u>two types</u> of crust — <u>continental</u> and <u>oceanic</u>:

> • <u>Continental crust</u> is <u>thicker</u> and <u>less dense</u>.
> • <u>Oceanic crust</u> is <u>thinner</u> and <u>more dense</u>.

5) The <u>plates</u> are <u>moving</u> because the rock in the <u>mantle underneath</u> them <u>is moving</u>.

6) The places where plates <u>meet</u> are called <u>boundaries</u> or <u>plate margins</u>:

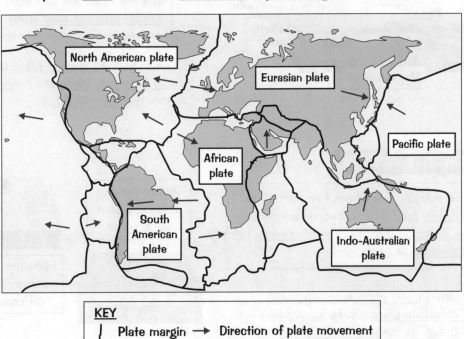

North American plate

Eurasian plate

Pacific plate

African plate

South American plate

Indo-Australian plate

KEY
| Plate margin → Direction of plate movement

Tectonic plates have to be washed by hand — they won't fit in the dishwasher...

Yes, I know this page isn't terribly exciting, but you need to understand the <u>Earth's structure</u> and what <u>tectonic plates</u> are or you'll really get your knickers in a twist later on in the section. Only carry on when your knickers are secure...

Types of Tectonic Plate Margins

Tectonic plate margins are places where plates meet. I like to think they have a cup of tea, a slice or two of cake and a natter about what's going on in the world. But in reality it's not so civilised...

There are Three Types of Plate Margin

1 DESTRUCTIVE MARGINS

Destructive margins are where two plates are moving towards each other.

- Where an oceanic plate meets a continental plate, the denser oceanic plate is forced down into the mantle and destroyed. This often creates volcanoes and ocean trenches (very deep sections of the ocean floor where the oceanic plate goes down).

- Where two continental plates meet, the plates smash together, but no crust is destroyed.

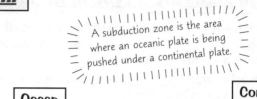

A subduction zone is the area where an oceanic plate is being pushed under a continental plate.

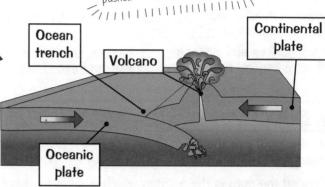

Ocean trench · Volcano · Continental plate · Oceanic plate

EXAMPLE: the Pacific plate is being forced under the Eurasian plate along the east coast of Japan.

The area where continental plates collide is called a collision zone.

2 CONSTRUCTIVE MARGINS

Constructive margins are where two plates are moving away from each other. Magma (molten rock) rises from the mantle to fill the gap and cools, creating new crust.

EXAMPLE: the Eurasian plate and the North American Plate are moving apart at the mid-Atlantic ridge.

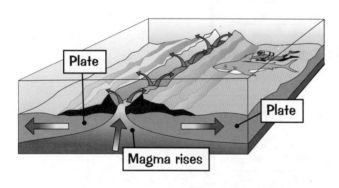

Plate · Plate · Magma rises

3 CONSERVATIVE MARGINS

Conservative margins are where two plates are moving sideways past each other, or are moving in the same direction but at different speeds. Crust isn't created or destroyed.

EXAMPLE: the Pacific plate is moving past the North American plate on the west coast of the USA, e.g. at the San Andreas fault.

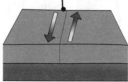

Plates moving sideways past each other

SLOW QUICK

Plates moving in the same direction at different speeds

I bet you thought this page was only going to be marginally interesting...

It's weird to think that the land you're sitting on as you read this book is moving around. You won't be able to notice it though because it's happening so slowly — but the plates have an occasional bout of attention seeking...

The Distribution of Tectonic Hazards

We're finally here, the juicy bit about earthquakes and volcanoes. There are three things to know about each hazard — which margins they occur at, where they happen and what causes them. Let learning commence.

Earthquakes Occur at All Three Types of Plate Margin

1) Earthquakes are caused by the pressure that builds up at all three types of plate margin:

Destructive margins — pressure builds up when one plate gets stuck as it's moving down past the other into the mantle.

Constructive margins — pressure builds along cracks within the plates as they move away from each other.

Conservative margins — pressure builds up when plates that are grinding past each other get stuck.

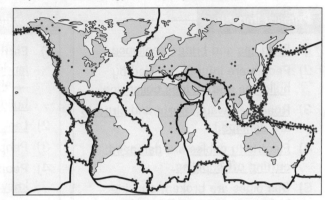

KEY
⬡ Earthquakes | Plate margin

2) The plates eventually jerk past each other, sending out shock waves (vibrations). These vibrations are the earthquake.

3) The shock waves spread out from the focus — the point in the Earth where the earthquake starts.

4) The epicentre is the point on the Earth's surface straight above the focus. Near the epicentre the shock waves are stronger and cause more damage.

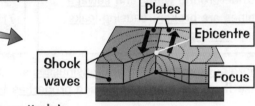

5) The amount of energy released by an earthquake (its magnitude) is measured using the Richter scale. The scale doesn't have an upper limit and it's logarithmic — this means an earthquake with a magnitude of 5 is ten times more powerful than one with a magnitude of 4.

Volcanoes are Found at Destructive and Constructive Plate Margins

1) At destructive plate margins the oceanic plate goes under the continental plate because it's more dense:

- The oceanic plate moves down into the mantle, where it's melted and destroyed.
- A pool of magma forms.
- The magma rises through cracks in the crust called vents.
- The magma erupts onto the surface (where it's called lava), forming a volcano.

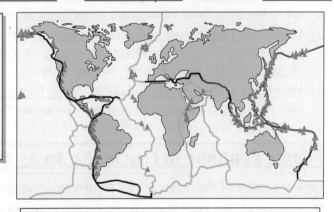

2) At constructive margins the magma rises up into the gap created by the plates moving apart, forming a volcano.

3) Some volcanoes also form over parts of the mantle that are really hot (called hotspots), e.g. in Hawaii.

KEY
🔺🔺🔺 Volcanoes
| Destructive plate margin | Constructive plate margin

Earthquakes are such jerks — volcanoes should learn not to rise to them....

I'd better say this now... don't be put off by any of the maps — you won't ever have to draw them. You should have a rough idea of where the hazards are though, so you don't put your foot in it and talk about volcanoes erupting in the UK.

Impacts of Earthquakes

Earthquakes make jelly wobble — but they have loads of more serious impacts...

Earthquakes have Primary and Secondary Impacts

The primary impacts of an earthquake are the immediate effects of the ground shaking. The secondary impacts are the effects that happen later on. Here are a few examples of the possible impacts:

Primary impacts

1) Buildings and bridges collapse.
2) People are injured or killed by buildings and bridges collapsing.
3) Roads, railways, ports and airports are damaged.
4) Electricity cables are damaged, cutting off supplies.
5) Gas pipes are broken, causing leaks and cutting off supplies.
6) Telephone poles and cables are destroyed.
7) Underground water and sewage pipes are broken, causing leaks and cutting off supplies.

Secondary impacts

1) Earthquakes can trigger landslides and tsunamis — these destroy more buildings and cause more injuries and deaths.
2) Leaking gas can be ignited, starting fires.
3) People are left homeless.
4) People may suffer psychological problems if they knew people who died or if they lose their home etc.
5) There's a shortage of clean water and a lack of proper sanitation — this makes it easier for diseases to spread.
6) Roads are blocked or destroyed so aid and emergency vehicles can't get through.
7) Businesses are damaged or destroyed, causing unemployment.

Tsunamis are a series of enormous waves caused when huge amounts of water get displaced, e.g. by tectonic plates moving quickly.

The more settlements built and businesses set up in an area, the greater the impact because there are more people and properties to be affected by an earthquake.

The Impacts of Earthquakes are More Severe in LEDCs

You need to know a few reasons why:

1) There's more poor quality housing in LEDCs. Poor quality houses are less stable, so they're destroyed more easily by earthquakes.
2) The infrastructure is often poorer in LEDCs. Poor quality roads make it harder for emergency services to reach injured people, which leads to more deaths.
3) LEDCs don't have much money to protect against earthquakes, e.g. by making buildings earthquake proof. They also don't have enough money or resources (e.g. food and emergency vehicles) to react straight away to earthquakes, so more people are affected by secondary impacts.
4) Healthcare is often worse in LEDCs. Many hospitals in LEDCs don't have enough supplies to deal with the large numbers of casualties after an earthquake, so more people die from treatable injuries.

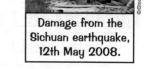

Damage from the Sichuan earthquake, 12th May 2008.

People Continue to Live in the Areas where Earthquakes Happen

Here are some of the reasons why people don't move away from earthquake prone areas, e.g. California:

1) They've always lived there — moving away would mean leaving friends and family.
2) They're employed in the area. If people move they would have to find new jobs.
3) They're confident of support from their government after an earthquake, e.g. to help rebuild houses.
4) Some people think that severe earthquakes won't happen again in the area, so it's safe to live there.

Some people just like living on the edge (of a plate)...

Earthquakes seem pretty exciting to the outsider, but they can be life-threatening for the people that experience them. All the different impacts affect both MEDCs and LEDCs, but they're more severe in LEDCs — you need to know why.

Reducing the Impacts of Earthquakes

Unfortunately earthquakes don't have an 'off' button, but the impacts they have can be reduced.

There are Many Ways of Reducing the Impacts of Earthquakes

Prediction

1) It's currently impossible to predict when an earthquake will happen. If you could, it would give people time to evacuate — this would reduce the number of injuries and deaths.

2) There can be clues that an earthquake is about to happen though. For example, lots of small tremors, cracks appearing in rocks and strange animal behaviour (e.g. rats abandoning nests).

3) It's possible to predict where future earthquakes may happen using data from past earthquakes, e.g. mapping where earthquakes have happened shows which places are likely to be affected again — these places can prepare themselves for the impacts of an earthquake.

Building techniques

1) Buildings can be designed to withstand earthquakes, e.g. by using materials like reinforced concrete or building special foundations that absorb an earthquake's energy.

2) Constructing earthquake-proof buildings reduces the number of buildings destroyed by an earthquake, so fewer people will be killed, injured, made homeless and made unemployed.

Planning

1) Future developments, e.g. new shopping centres, can be planned to avoid the areas most at risk from earthquakes. This reduces the number of buildings destroyed by an earthquake.

2) Firebreaks can be made to reduce the spread of fires (a secondary impact, see previous page).

3) Emergency services can train and prepare for disasters, e.g. by practising rescuing people from collapsed buildings and by stockpiling medicine. This reduces the number of people killed.

4) Governments can plan evacuation routes to get people out of dangerous areas quickly and safely after an earthquake. This reduces the number of people killed or injured by things like fires.

Education

1) Governments and other organisations can educate people about what to do if there's an earthquake (e.g. stand in a doorway) and how to evacuate. This reduces deaths.

2) People can be told how to make a survival kit containing things like food, water, a torch, a radio and batteries. The kits reduce the chances of people dying if they're stuck in the area.

Aid

1) LEDCs that have been affected by earthquakes can receive aid from governments or organisations — it can be things like food, water, money or people (e.g. doctors or rescuers).

2) Aid helps to reduce the impacts, e.g. money aid is used to rebuild homes, reducing homelessness.

Some Strategies are More Sustainable than Others

Sustainable strategies meet the needs of people today without stopping people in the future meeting their needs. A strategy is not sustainable if it's not effective, as it doesn't meet the needs of people today. A strategy is also not sustainable if it's expensive or it harms the environment, as it stops people in the future meeting their needs. Here's a bit on the sustainability of strategies to reduce the impact of earthquakes:

1) Predicting earthquakes is not an effective strategy, so it's not sustainable.

2) The other strategies above are sustainable — they're all effective and environmentally friendly, but some are more sustainable than others.

3) The ones that are more sustainable are basically the more cost-effective ones, e.g. good planning is usually more effective than aid at reducing impacts and it's much cheaper.

4) Some strategies are expensive (e.g. constructing earthquake-proof buildings), but they can be more sustainable than other strategies because in the long term less money and resources are used rebuilding.

I'd reduce the impacts by making everything out of rubber — everything...

If you could predict exactly when an earthquake will happen you'd make yourself a lot of friends, but top scientists think it's just too difficult to do. Anyway, make sure you know about the other strategies too and their sustainability.

Earthquakes — Case Studies

And you thought I'd forgotten all about the case studies. This page is about earthquakes, but if you've done about volcanoes that's OK — just make sure you know one example in an LEDC and one in an MEDC.

MEDCs and LEDCs are Affected Differently by Earthquakes

The impacts of earthquakes are different in different parts of the world. A lot depends on how wealthy the part of the world is. I'd bet my budgie that they'll want you to compare a hazard in an MEDC with one in an LEDC in the exam:

Earthquake in an MEDC:

Place: L'Aquila, Italy
Date: 6th April, 2009
Size: 6.3 on the Richter Scale
Cause: Movement along a crack in the plate at a destructive margin.
Cost of damage: Around $15 billion

Earthquake in an LEDC:

Place: Kashmir, Pakistan
Date: 8th October, 2005
Size: 7.6 on the Richter Scale
Cause: Movement along a crack in the plate at a destructive margin.
Cost of damage: Around $5 billion

Primary impacts

- Around 290 deaths, mostly from collapsed buildings.
- Hundreds of people were injured.
- Thousands of buildings were damaged or destroyed.
- A bridge near the town of Fossa collapsed, and a mains water pipe was broken near the town of Paganica.

- Around 80 000 deaths, mostly from collapsed buildings.
- Hundreds of thousands of people injured.
- Entire villages and thousands of buildings were destroyed.
- Water pipelines and electricity lines were broken, cutting off supply.

Secondary impacts

- Aftershocks (smaller earthquakes that happen after the main one) hampered rescue efforts and caused more damage.
- Thousands of people were made homeless.
- Fires in some collapsed buildings caused more damage.
- The broken water pipe near the town of Paganica caused a landslide.

- Landslides buried buildings and people. They also blocked access roads and cut off water supplies, electricity supplies and telephone lines.
- Around 3 million people were made homeless.
- Diarrhoea and other diseases spread due to little clean water.
- Freezing winter conditions shortly after the earthquake caused more casualties and meant rescue and rebuilding operations were difficult.

Reasons for severity of impacts

- Ambulances, fire engines and the army were sent in to rescue survivors. Cranes and diggers were used to remove rubble. This reduced the number of people killed because injured people were rescued quickly.
- International teams with rescue dogs were sent in, also reducing the number of people killed.
- Camps were set up for homeless people with water, food and medical care. This reduced homelessness and injured people were treated.
- There are laws on construction standards in Italy so some buildings were built to withstand earthquakes and didn't collapse. This reduced the number of people killed. However, some modern buildings weren't built to the right standard. This increased the number of people killed and the cost of the damage because buildings collapsed that should have been protected.
- Italy has a Civil Protection Department that trains volunteers to help with things like rescue operations. This helped reduce the impacts.

- Buildings weren't designed to withstand earthquakes. This increased the number of people killed and the cost of the damage because loads of buildings collapsed.
- There were few roads and they were badly constructed, so help didn't arrive in many areas for days or weeks. People had to be rescued by hand without any equipment or help from emergency services. This increased the number of people killed because injured people weren't rescued quickly enough. International aid and rescue teams eventually arrived though, so other injured people were helped, which reduced the number of people killed.
- Tents, blankets and medical supplies were distributed within a month, but not to all areas affected. This reduced homelessness and injured people were treated, but only in the areas that got the help.

I'd wet myself if I was in an earthquake — regardless of the country I was in...

The amount of damage an earthquake does, and the number of people that get hurt is different in different parts of the world. You need to know a couple of good examples for your exam, one from an LEDC and one from an MEDC.

Impacts of Volcanoes

Volcanoes usually look like mountains... until they <u>explode</u> and throw <u>molten rock</u> everywhere. Honestly, they've got such a temper, though I'd probably be in a bad mood if I was sitting on a load of <u>magma</u>.

Lots of People Live Close to Volcanoes

The <u>reasons why</u> people <u>continue</u> to <u>live around volcanoes</u> despite the hazards are <u>exactly</u> the <u>same</u> as <u>why people keep living</u> in <u>areas prone</u> to <u>earthquakes</u> (see p. 52). But there are a <u>few reasons</u> <u>why</u> people <u>choose</u> to <u>live close</u> to <u>volcanoes</u>:

1) The <u>soil around volcanoes</u> is <u>fertile</u> because it's full of <u>minerals</u> from <u>volcanic</u> <u>ash</u> and <u>lava</u>. This makes it <u>good</u> for <u>growing crops</u>, which <u>attracts farmers</u>.

2) <u>Volcanoes</u> are <u>tourist attractions</u> — <u>loads</u> of <u>tourists visit volcanoes</u> so lots of people <u>live around volcanoes</u> to <u>work</u> in the <u>tourist industry</u>.

3) <u>Volcanoes</u> are a <u>source</u> of <u>geothermal energy</u>, which can be used to <u>generate</u> <u>electricity</u>. So people <u>live around volcanoes</u> to <u>work</u> at <u>power stations</u>.

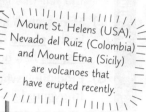
Mount St. Helens (USA), Nevado del Ruiz (Colombia) and Mount Etna (Sicily) are volcanoes that have erupted recently.

Volcanic Eruptions have Primary and Secondary Impacts

The <u>primary impacts</u> of a <u>volcanic eruption</u> are the <u>immediate effects</u> of a volcano spewing out <u>lava</u>, <u>ash</u>, <u>rocks</u> and <u>gas</u> (e.g. carbon dioxide and sulphur dioxide), as well as <u>pyroclastic flows</u>. The <u>secondary impacts</u> are the effects that happen <u>later on</u>.

Here are a <u>few examples</u> of the <u>possible impacts</u>:

Pyroclastic flows are extremely fast moving flows of ash, rock and gas that move down the sides of a volcano.

Primary impacts

1) <u>Buildings</u> and <u>roads</u> are <u>destroyed</u> by <u>lava</u> <u>flows</u> and <u>pyroclastic flows</u> — buildings also <u>collapse</u> if <u>enough ash falls on them</u>.

2) <u>People</u> and <u>animals</u> are <u>injured</u> or <u>killed</u>, mainly by <u>pyroclastic flows</u> but also by <u>lava flows</u> and <u>falling rocks</u>.

3) <u>Crops</u> are <u>damaged</u> and <u>water supplies</u> are <u>contaminated</u> when <u>ash</u> falls on them.

4) <u>People</u>, <u>animals</u> and <u>plants</u> are <u>suffocated</u> by <u>carbon dioxide</u>.

Secondary impacts

1) <u>Mudflows</u> (also called <u>lahars</u>) form when <u>volcanic material mixes</u> with <u>water</u>, e.g. from <u>heavy rainfall</u> or <u>snow melt</u>. Mudflows cause <u>loads more destruction</u>, <u>deaths</u> and <u>injuries</u>.

2) <u>Fires</u> are <u>started</u> by <u>lava flows</u> and <u>pyroclastic flows</u>, which then <u>spread</u>.

3) People may suffer <u>psychological problems</u> if they <u>knew people who died</u> or if they <u>lose their home</u> etc.

4) People are left <u>homeless</u>.

5) There's a <u>shortage</u> of <u>food</u> because <u>crops</u> are <u>damaged</u>.

6) There's a <u>shortage</u> of <u>clean water</u>.

7) <u>Roads</u> are <u>blocked</u> or <u>destroyed</u> so <u>aid</u> and <u>emergency vehicles</u> <u>can't get through</u>.

8) <u>Businesses</u> are <u>damaged</u> or <u>destroyed</u>, causing <u>unemployment</u>.

9) <u>Sulphur dioxide</u> released into the atmosphere causes <u>acid rain</u>.

BERNHARD EDMAIER / SCIENCE PHOTO LIBRARY

This was the city of Plymouth in Montserrat (an LEDC) — it was buried under ash and mud after a volcanic eruption in 1997.

The impacts of volcanic eruptions are <u>more severe</u> in <u>LEDCs</u> than in MEDCs for exactly the <u>same reasons</u> <u>why earthquakes</u> are <u>more severe</u> in <u>LEDCs</u> — have a look back at page 52.

Studying volcanoes — what a blast...

Volcanoes like to <u>throw up lava</u> without bothering to rush to the toilet. To be fair though, they'd just melt the bowl.
Volcanic eruptions cause <u>various nasty impacts</u> and you've got to be clear on which are <u>primary</u> and which are <u>secondary</u>.

Reducing the Impacts of Volcanoes

It's <u>impossible</u> to <u>stop</u> a volcano erupting — not even with a humongous bath plug. But a few people have come up with <u>ideas</u> to <u>reduce</u> the <u>impacts</u> of <u>volcanic eruptions</u> as much as possible, which is nice of them.

There are Many Ways of Reducing the Impacts of Volcanic Eruptions

Prediction

1) Unlike earthquakes, it's <u>possible</u> to <u>roughly predict when</u> a <u>volcanic eruption</u> will happen. Scientists can <u>monitor</u> the tell-tale <u>signs</u> that come <u>before</u> a <u>volcanic eruption</u>.

2) Things such as <u>tiny earthquakes</u>, <u>escaping gas</u>, and <u>changes</u> in the <u>shape</u> of the volcano (e.g. <u>bulges</u> in the land where <u>magma</u> has <u>built up</u> under it) all mean an <u>eruption</u> is <u>likely</u>.

3) Predicting when a volcano is going to erupt <u>gives people time</u> to <u>evacuate</u> — this <u>reduces</u> the number of <u>injuries</u> and <u>deaths</u>.

Uh oh...

Planning

1) <u>Future developments</u>, e.g. new houses, can be <u>planned</u> to <u>avoid</u> the <u>areas most at risk</u> from volcanic eruptions. This <u>reduces</u> the number of <u>buildings destroyed</u> by an eruption.

2) <u>Firebreaks</u> can be made to <u>reduce</u> the <u>spread of fires</u>.

3) <u>Emergency services</u> can <u>train</u> and <u>prepare</u> for disasters, e.g. by practising setting up emergency camps for homeless people. This <u>reduces</u> the number of <u>people killed</u>.

4) Governments can plan <u>evacuation routes</u> to <u>get people away from the volcano quickly</u> and <u>safely</u>. This <u>reduces</u> the number of <u>people injured</u> or <u>killed</u> by things like <u>pyroclastic flows</u> or <u>mudflows</u>.

Building techniques

1) Buildings <u>can't be designed</u> to <u>withstand lava flows</u> or <u>pyroclastic flows</u>, but they can be <u>strengthened</u> so they're <u>less likely</u> to <u>collapse under</u> the <u>weight</u> of <u>falling ash</u>.

2) The lava from some volcanoes can be <u>diverted away from buildings</u> using <u>barriers</u>.

3) Both of these <u>reduce</u> the number of <u>buildings destroyed</u>, so <u>fewer people</u> will be <u>killed</u>, <u>injured</u>, <u>made homeless</u> and <u>made unemployed</u>.

Education

1) <u>Governments</u> and other <u>organisations</u> can <u>educate people</u> about <u>how to evacuate</u> if a volcano erupts. This helps people <u>get out of danger quickly</u> and safely, which <u>reduces deaths</u>.

2) People can be <u>told how</u> to <u>make</u> a <u>survival kit</u> containing things like <u>food</u>, <u>water</u>, a <u>torch</u>, a <u>radio</u>, <u>batteries</u> and <u>dust masks</u>. The kits <u>reduce</u> the <u>chance</u> of <u>people dying</u> if they're <u>stuck</u> in the <u>area</u>.

Aid

1) <u>LEDCs</u> that have been <u>affected</u> by a <u>volcanic eruption</u> can <u>receive aid</u> from <u>governments</u> or <u>organisations</u> — it can be things like <u>food</u>, <u>water</u>, <u>money</u> or <u>people</u> (e.g. doctors).

2) Aid helps to <u>reduce</u> the <u>impacts</u>, e.g. <u>food aid stops people going hungry</u>.

Some Strategies are More Sustainable than Others

There's a <u>definition</u> of a sustainable strategy back on p. 53. You need to know a bit about the sustainability of strategies to reduce the impact of volcanic eruptions:

1) <u>All</u> of the strategies <u>are sustainable</u> because <u>they're all effective</u> and <u>environmentally friendly</u>.

2) Some are <u>more cost-effective</u> than others though, so are <u>more sustainable</u>.

3) <u>Predicting eruptions</u> needs <u>special equipment</u> and <u>trained scientists</u>, which makes it <u>expensive</u>, but if it's accurate it saves a lot of lives.

4) <u>Building techniques</u> can be <u>very expensive</u>, but can <u>save money</u> if they <u>stop building destruction</u>.

The section's ended with a bang...

...and just in time too — I'd completely run out of puns along the 'smashing, blast, bang' theme. It's been a section filled with danger and flying rocks, and I think I need a bit of a lie down. However, there's the matter of a <u>few questions</u>...

Revision Summary for Section Five

What a cracking section, earth-shattering one might say (thought of a few more puns after all). It may be a section about hazards, but have a go at these questions and the exam will rapidly become less of one. I know it looks like there's a lot here, but you'll be surprised at just how much you learnt. Try a few at a time and then check the answers by looking back at the pages. Once you can answer them all standing on your head and juggling five balls, move on to the next section — where we head to the skies...

1) What is a natural hazard?

2) Describe the Earth's structure.

3) What are the places where tectonic plates meet called?

4) Describe what happens when an oceanic plate meets a continental plate at a destructive margin.

5) What happens at constructive margins?

6) Describe one way that tectonic plates move at conservative margins.

7) What is an earthquake caused by?

8) What is the name of the point in the Earth where an earthquake starts?

9) a) Name the two types of plate margin that volcanoes are found at.

   b) Describe how a volcano is formed at one of the margins.

10) What is the difference between the primary impacts and the secondary impacts of an earthquake?

11) Give three examples of a primary impact of an earthquake.

12) Give three examples of a secondary impact of an earthquake.

13) Describe two reasons why the impacts of an earthquake are more severe in LEDCs.

14) Give two reasons why people continue to live in areas where earthquakes happen.

15) Describe one way buildings can be designed to withstand an earthquake.

16) Describe how education can reduce the impacts of earthquakes.

17) Why is prediction not a sustainable strategy for reducing the impacts of an earthquake?

18) a) Name an LEDC and an MEDC where an earthquake or volcanic eruption caused a disaster.

   b) Describe two primary impacts and two secondary impacts of each disaster.

   c) Explain why the severity of the impacts was different in the two places.

19) Give two reasons why people choose to live close to volcanoes.

20) Give three examples of a primary impact of a volcanic eruption.

21) Give three examples of a secondary impact of a volcanic eruption.

22) How do scientists try to predict volcanic eruptions?

23) Describe two planning strategies that reduce the impact of a volcanic eruption.

24) Describe two building techniques that reduce the impact of a volcanic eruption.

Tropical Storms

As if that last section wasn't hazardous enough, this one has a shed load more hazards... well, two more, but I exaggerate when I get excited (and I get excited by the strangest things, like hazards... and bubbles).

Climatic Hazards are Hazards Caused By the Weather

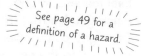
See page 49 for a definition of a hazard.

1) Climatic hazards include tropical storms and droughts.

2) First up is tropical storms — these are intense low pressure weather systems. They've got lots of different names (hurricanes, typhoons and tropical cyclones), but they're all the same thing.

Tropical Storms Develop over Warm Water

Tropical storms are huge storms with strong winds and torrential rain. Scientists don't know exactly how they're formed, but they know where they form and some of the conditions that are needed:

1) Tropical storms develop above sea water that's 27 °C or higher.

2) They happen when sea temperatures are highest, so they happen at different times in different places. For example, tropical storm season is August to October in the Atlantic, and May to December in the north east Pacific.

3) Warm, moist air rises and condensation occurs. This releases huge amounts of energy, which makes the storms really powerful.

4) They move west because of the easterly winds near the equator.

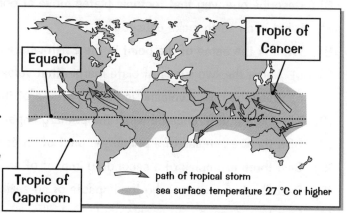

path of tropical storm
sea surface temperature 27 °C or higher

5) They lose strength as they move over land because the energy supply from the warm water is cut off.

6) Most tropical storms occur between 5° and 30° north and south of the equator, e.g. in the Atlantic and the Indian Ocean (any further from the equator and the water isn't warm enough).

You Need to Learn the Characteristics of Tropical Storms

1) Tropical storms spin anticlockwise and move north west (in the northern hemisphere).

2) They're circular in shape and can be hundreds of kilometres wide.

3) They usually last between 7 and 14 days.

4) The centre of the storm's called the eye — it's up to 50 km across and is caused by descending air. There's very low pressure, light winds, no clouds and no rain in the eye.

5) The eye is surrounded by the eyewall, where there's spiralling rising air, very strong winds (around 160 km per hour), storm clouds and torrential rain.

6) Towards the edges of the storm the wind speed falls, the clouds become smaller and more scattered, and the rain becomes less intense.

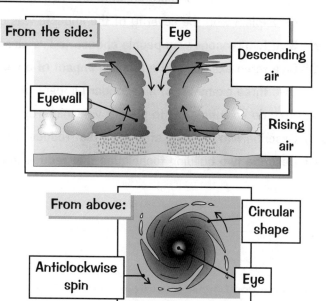

Forget warm water, you're in hot water when one of these turns up...

Well, that blew the cobwebs away. Since all the top scientists haven't worked it out yet, you don't need to know exactly how a tropical storm forms, you just need to know where they're found, why they're found there and their characteristics.

Impacts of Tropical Storms

Tropical storms try really hard to make an <u>impact</u>. Unfortunately, no-one ever appreciates their effort...

Tropical Storms *have Primary and Secondary Impacts*

The <u>primary impacts</u> of a <u>tropical storm</u> are the <u>immediate effects</u> of <u>strong winds</u>, <u>high rainfall</u> and <u>storm surges</u>. The <u>secondary impacts</u> are the effects that happen <u>later on</u>. Here are a <u>few examples</u> of the <u>possible impacts</u>:

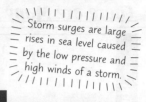
Storm surges are large rises in sea level caused by the low pressure and high winds of a storm.

Primary impacts

1) <u>Buildings</u> and <u>bridges</u> are <u>destroyed</u>.

2) <u>Rivers</u> and <u>coastal areas flood</u>.

Damage from Hurricane Katrina, 29th August 2005.

3) People <u>drown</u>, or they're <u>injured</u> or <u>killed</u> by <u>debris</u> that's <u>blown around</u>.

4) <u>Roads</u>, <u>railways</u>, <u>ports</u> and <u>airports</u> are <u>damaged</u>.

5) <u>Electricity cables</u> are <u>damaged</u>, <u>cutting off supplies</u>.

6) <u>Telephone poles</u> and <u>cables</u> are <u>destroyed</u>.

7) <u>Sewage overflows</u> due to flooding. The sewage often <u>contaminates water supplies</u>.

8) <u>Crops</u> are <u>damaged</u> and <u>livestock</u> is <u>killed</u>.

9) Heavy rain makes <u>hills unstable</u>, causing <u>landslides</u>.

10) <u>Beaches</u> are <u>eroded</u> and <u>coastal habitats</u> (e.g. coral reefs) are <u>damaged</u>.

Secondary impacts

1) People are left <u>homeless</u>.

2) There's a <u>shortage</u> of <u>clean water</u> and a <u>lack</u> of proper <u>sanitation</u> — this makes it <u>easier</u> for <u>diseases</u> to <u>spread</u>.

3) <u>Roads</u> are <u>blocked</u> or <u>destroyed</u> so <u>aid</u> and <u>emergency vehicles</u> <u>can't get through</u>.

4) <u>Businesses</u> are <u>damaged</u> or <u>destroyed</u>, causing <u>unemployment</u>.

5) There's a <u>shortage</u> of <u>food</u> because <u>crops</u> are <u>damaged</u> and <u>livestock</u> has <u>died</u>.

6) People may suffer <u>psychological problems</u> if they <u>knew people who died</u>.

The <u>more settlements</u> built and <u>businesses</u> set up <u>in an area</u>, the <u>greater</u> the <u>impact</u> because there are <u>more people</u> and <u>properties</u> to be <u>affected by a tropical storm</u>.

The Impacts of Tropical Storms *are More Severe in LEDCs*

You need to know a few <u>reasons</u> why:

1) There's <u>more poor quality housing</u> in LEDCs. Poor quality houses are <u>destroyed more easily</u> by strong winds and flooding.

2) The <u>infrastructure</u> is often <u>poorer</u> in LEDCs. <u>Poor quality roads</u> make it <u>harder</u> for <u>emergency services</u> to <u>rescue people</u>, which leads to <u>more deaths</u>.

3) <u>More people</u> in LEDCs <u>depend on farming</u>. If <u>crops</u> and <u>livestock</u> are <u>destroyed</u> <u>lots</u> of people will <u>lose their livelihoods</u>, and some might <u>starve</u>.

4) LEDCs <u>don't have much money</u> to <u>protect</u> against tropical storms, e.g. by building flood defences. They also <u>don't have enough money</u> or <u>resources</u> (e.g. food and helicopters) to <u>react straight away</u> to tropical storms, so <u>more people</u> are <u>affected</u> by <u>secondary impacts</u>.

5) <u>Healthcare</u> is often <u>worse</u> in LEDCs. <u>Many hospitals</u> in LEDCs <u>don't have enough supplies</u> to deal with the <u>large numbers of casualties</u> after a tropical storm, so more <u>people die</u> from <u>treatable injuries</u>.

People Continue to Live *in the Areas where Tropical Storms Happen*

The <u>reasons</u> why people <u>don't move away</u> from <u>areas</u> that are <u>prone</u> to tropical storms are the same as why people don't move away from areas prone to earthquakes (see p. 52) — they <u>don't want to leave friends</u>, they've got a <u>job in the area</u>, they <u>don't</u> think a tropical storm <u>will happen again</u> so it's <u>safe</u> etc.

Getting smacked in the face by a wet fish — a rare impact of tropical storms...

Tropical storms pretty much <u>wreak havoc</u> in the areas they hit — boats get tossed into trees, hills go for a slide and the winds are so strong you can't stand upright... you want to get out of there faster than Superman in a kryptonite mine.

Section Six — Climatic Hazards

Reducing the Impacts of Tropical Storms

I think I'm psychic — I just knew this page was going to be about reducing the impacts of tropical storms.

There are Many Ways of Reducing the Impacts of Tropical Storms

Prediction

1) When and where tropical storms will hit land can be predicted. Scientists use data from things like radar, satellites and aircraft to track the storm. Computer models are then used to calculate a predicted path for the storm.

2) Predicting where and when a tropical storm is going to happen gives people time to evacuate — this reduces the number of injuries and deaths. It also gives them time to protect their homes and businesses, e.g. by boarding up windows so they don't get smashed.

©iStockphoto.com

Planning

1) Future developments, e.g. new houses, can be planned to avoid the areas most at risk (e.g. right on the coast). This reduces the number of buildings destroyed by winds or flooding.

2) Emergency services can train and prepare for disasters, e.g. by practising rescuing people from flooded areas with helicopters. This reduces the number of people killed.

3) Governments can plan evacuation routes to get people away from storms quickly. This reduces the number of people injured or killed by things like flying debris or floodwater.

A hurricane evacuation route sign in Florida, USA.

Building techniques

1) Buildings can be designed to withstand tropical storms, e.g. by using reinforced concrete or by fixing roofs securely so they don't get blown off. Buildings can also be put on stilts so they're safe from floodwater.

2) Flood defences can be built along rivers (e.g. levees) and coasts (e.g. sea walls).

3) All of these reduce the number of buildings destroyed, so fewer people will be killed, injured, made homeless and made unemployed.

Education

1) Governments and other organisations can educate people about how to prepare for a tropical storm (e.g. by stockpiling water and food) and how to evacuate. This helps reduce deaths.

2) People can be told how to make a survival kit containing things like food, water and medication. The kits reduce the chance of people dying if they're stuck in the area.

Aid

Governments or organisations often send aid to countries hit by tropical storms, e.g. food, bottled water, tents. This helps to reduce the impacts, e.g. food aid stops people going hungry.

Some Strategies are More Sustainable than Others

There's a definition of a sustainable strategy way back on p. 53.
Here's a bit on the sustainability of strategies to reduce the impact of tropical storms:

1) All of the strategies are sustainable because they're all effective and environmentally friendly.

2) Some are more cost-effective than others though, so are more sustainable.

3) Predicting tropical storms needs special equipment (e.g. radars) and trained scientists, which makes it expensive, but if it's accurate it saves a lot of lives.

4) Building techniques can be very expensive, but can save a lot of money if they stop building destruction.

I predict you'll need aid if you don't get learning this page...

Prediction means you know if you have to do some serious plywood DIY and hightail it out of there. Good evacuation planning means you can hightail quickly and safely. Other things help make sure you've got a house to come back to.

Tropical Storms — Case Studies

Here are a couple of <u>case studies</u> on all things stormy. I worry I spoil you, but I think you deserve a treat. If you know two drought case studies really well you can use those in the exam instead.

MEDCs <u>and</u> LEDCs <u>are</u> Affected Differently <u>by</u> Tropical Storms

The <u>impacts</u> of tropical storms are <u>different</u> in different parts of the world. A lot depends on how <u>wealthy</u> the part of the world is. Here are a couple of <u>case studies</u>, so you can cash in on those marks when you get asked to <u>compare</u> two case studies in the exam.

Tropical storm in an <u>MEDC</u>:

<u>Name</u>: Hurricane Katrina
<u>Place</u>: South east USA
<u>Date</u>: 29th August, 2005
<u>Cost of damage</u>: around $300 billion

Tropical storm in an <u>LEDC</u>:

<u>Name</u>: Cyclone Nargis
<u>Place</u>: Irrawaddy delta, Burma
<u>Date</u>: 2nd May, 2008
<u>Cost of damage</u>: around $4 billion

Primary impacts

- More than <u>1800 people</u> were <u>killed</u>.
- <u>300 000 houses</u> were <u>destroyed</u>.
- <u>3 million people</u> were left <u>without electricity</u>.
- <u>One</u> of the <u>main routes</u> out of New Orleans was <u>closed</u> because parts of the <u>I-10 bridge collapsed</u>.
- <u>Coastal habitats</u> such as <u>sea turtle breeding beaches</u> were <u>damaged</u>.

- More than <u>140 000 people</u> were <u>killed</u>.
- <u>450 000 houses</u> were <u>destroyed</u>.
- <u>1700 schools</u> were <u>destroyed</u>.
- <u>200 000 farm animals</u> were <u>killed</u>, <u>crops</u> were lost and over <u>40%</u> of <u>food stores</u> were <u>destroyed</u>.
- <u>Coastal habitats</u> such as <u>mangrove forests</u> were <u>damaged</u>.

Secondary impacts

- <u>Tens of thousands</u> of people were made <u>homeless</u>.
- <u>230 000 jobs were lost</u> from businesses that were <u>damaged</u> or <u>destroyed</u>.
- <u>Water supplies</u> were <u>polluted</u> with <u>sewage</u>, <u>chemicals</u> and <u>dead bodies</u>.

- <u>2-3 million people</u> were made <u>homeless</u>.
- <u>Millions of people</u> lost their <u>livelihoods</u>.
- <u>Over 70%</u> of households <u>didn't have access</u> to <u>clean water</u>.

Reasons for severity of impacts

- The <u>USA</u> has a sophisticated <u>monitoring system</u> to <u>predict</u> if a <u>hurricane</u> will hit (e.g. by using <u>satellite images</u> of the Atlantic) — so <u>people were warned</u>. <u>70-80%</u> of New Orleans residents were <u>evacuated before</u> the hurricane reached land. This <u>reduced</u> the number of <u>people killed</u> because lots of people had <u>left</u> the <u>areas</u> where the <u>tropical storm hit</u>.
- <u>Mississippi</u> and <u>Louisiana</u> declared <u>states of emergency</u> on <u>26th August</u> — they set up <u>control centres</u> and <u>stockpiled supplies</u>. This helped to <u>reduce</u> the <u>impacts</u>.
- The <u>coastguard</u>, <u>police</u>, <u>fire service</u> and <u>army rescued</u> over <u>50 000 people</u>. This <u>reduced</u> the number of <u>people killed</u> because people were <u>rescued</u>.
- <u>Flood defences</u> that were supposed to <u>protect</u> New Orleans failed. This <u>increased</u> the number of <u>people killed</u> and the <u>cost</u> of the <u>damage</u> because <u>flooding</u> in the area was <u>worse</u> than it <u>should have been</u>.

- <u>Indian</u> and <u>Thai weather agencies warned</u> the <u>Burmese Government</u> that Cyclone Nargis was <u>likely</u> to hit the country. Despite this, <u>Burmese forecasters</u> reported there was <u>little or no risk</u>. This <u>increased</u> the number of <u>people killed</u> because <u>people weren't evacuated</u> in time, despite the warnings.
- There were <u>no emergency</u> or <u>evacuation plans</u>.
- Burma's <u>Government</u> initially <u>refused</u> to accept any <u>foreign aid</u>. <u>Aid workers</u> were only <u>allowed in 3 weeks after</u> the disaster occurred. This <u>increased</u> the number of <u>people killed</u> because <u>help</u> for <u>some injured people</u> came <u>too late</u>.
- <u>Aid</u> from many countries was <u>eventually accepted</u>, e.g. <u>32 tonnes</u> of aid from <u>India</u>, including <u>tents</u>, <u>blankets</u> and <u>medicine</u>. This <u>reduced</u> the number of <u>people that died</u> from things like starvation.

<u>Katrina — sounds like a nice girl...</u>

When you compare the two, you can see that the <u>impacts</u> were <u>way worse</u> in <u>Burma</u>, and they were <u>much better prepared</u> in the <u>USA</u>. Make sure you <u>learn both</u> case studies though — then you'll blow 'em away in the exam.

Drought

I bet you're wondering when all this hazard malarkey is going to end. Well, you're in luck because drought's the last hazard you need to know about. But don't get too excited yet — there are still three pages to go...

Drought *is when Conditions* are Drier than Normal

1) A drought is a long period (weeks, months or years) when rainfall is below average.

2) Water supplies, e.g. lakes and rivers, are depleted during a drought because people keep using them but they aren't replenished by rainfall. Also, droughts are often accompanied by high temperatures, which increase the rate of evaporation, so water supplies are depleted faster.

3) The length of a drought is different in different places, e.g. the worst drought in Britain since records began lasted 16 months, whilst droughts in African countries can last for more than a decade.

4) You need to know about the climatic conditions that cause periods of drought:

> 1) Droughts are caused when changes in atmospheric circulation mean it doesn't rain much in an area for years, e.g. this happens in Ethiopia.
>
> 2) Changes in atmospheric circulation can also make the annual rains fail (e.g. monsoon rains don't come when they normally do in places like India).
>
> 3) Droughts are also caused when high pressure weather systems (called anticyclones) block depressions (weather systems that cause rain), e.g. this happens in the UK.

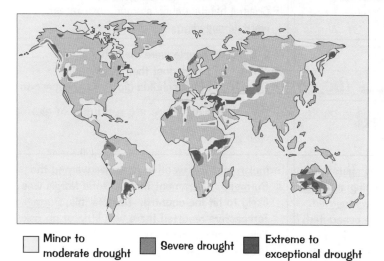

5) The map on the left shows the areas of the world that were affected by drought in November 2008.

6) Areas most at risk from drought are north-eastern Africa, the Sahel, southern Africa, the Middle East, Australia and parts of eastern South America and Indonesia.

☐ Minor to moderate drought   ▨ Severe drought   ▪ Extreme to exceptional drought

People Continue to Live in the Areas where Droughts Happen

The reasons why people don't move away from areas that are prone to droughts are similar to why people don't move away from areas prone to earthquakes (see p. 52) — they've always lived there, they've got a job in the area, they don't think a drought will happen again soon etc.

©iStockphoto.com/Klaas Lingbeek-van Kranen

Droughts are quite sarcastic — they have a dry sense of humour...

Now you know what droughts are and how they happen. If you don't, then you've come to the wrong place — this book is most useful if you work your way down pages, from top to bottom. It's an easy mistake to make though...

Impacts of Droughts

I know what you're thinking — 'please, no more hazard impacts'. Your wish is my command (after this page).

Droughts have Primary and Secondary Impacts

The primary impacts of droughts are the immediate effects of low rainfall and reduced water supplies. Secondary impacts are the effects that happen later on. Here are some examples of the possible impacts:

Primary impacts

1) Vegetation dies (including crops).
2) People and animals die from dehydration.
3) Aquatic animals (e.g. fish) die because lakes and rivers dry up.
4) Soil dries out and is easily eroded by the wind and rain.

©iStockphoto.com/Morley Read

Secondary impacts

1) Animals die from starvation because there's no vegetation.
2) There's a shortage of food because crops have failed and livestock has died, so people die from starvation.
3) Soil erosion is increased because there's less vegetation to hold it together. This causes desertification — where land becomes unsuitable for growing vegetation.
4) There are conflicts over water supplies.
5) People move out of the area to find water.
6) Farms close, causing unemployment.
7) People may suffer psychological problems, e.g. stress from losing their business.
8) Dried out vegetation can be easily ignited, e.g. by lightning, causing wildfires.
9) Winds pick up dry soil, causing dust storms.

Some Human Activities Increase the Impacts of Droughts

Some of the things that humans do make the impacts of droughts worse. Here are a couple of examples:

Overgrazing

Overgrazing reduces vegetation in an area. This makes the soil erosion caused by droughts even worse — with fewer plants, soil isn't held together as strongly so it's eroded more easily.

As usual, the more settlements built and farms set up in an area, the greater the impacts because there are more people and businesses to be affected by drought.

Excessive irrigation

Irrigation is where water is artificially supplied from rivers or lakes to farmland to increase crop production. However, excessive irrigation depletes rivers and lakes, which increases the impact of drought because there's less water. Also, when irrigation water evaporates, salts are left in the soil (this is salinisation). Crops don't grow well in salty soil, so this also increases the impact of drought.

The Impacts of Droughts are More Severe in LEDCs

Droughts happen all over the world, but they have a greater impact in LEDCs. You need to know why:

1) More people in LEDCs depend on farming. If crops and livestock die lots of people will lose their livelihoods and some might starve.
2) LEDCs have less money to prepare for droughts or respond to them, e.g. they can't afford to build reservoirs (see the next page), so the impacts of a drought are more severe.

Make no bones about it — the impacts of drought aren't that great...

The stuff on this page isn't too tricky so it'll be nice and easy to store it in your memory box. Make sure you know all about the two human activities that make the impacts of drought a lot worse. Silly humans, when will they learn...

Reducing the Impacts of Droughts

Luckily there are ways to reduce the impacts of droughts. Some of them are more sophisticated than my rain dance (a cross between the moonwalk and the funky chicken) and surprisingly they work much better.

There are Many Ways of Reducing the Impacts of Droughts

Prediction

1) Droughts can be predicted a short time before they happen by monitoring rainfall, soil moisture and river levels.

2) When a drought is predicted, things can be done to reduce the impacts, e.g. banning hosepipes, rationing water or moving people out of areas that will be worst affected.

Water conservation

1) People can conserve water by reducing the amount they use in their homes, e.g. by installing low volume flush toilets, and by having showers instead of baths.

2) People can also install water butts at home to collect rainwater and use it to wash their car or water their garden.

3) These reduce the demand on water supplies, so more water is available during a drought.

Farming techniques

1) Drought-resistant crops (ones that need little water) can be grown, e.g. millet, sorghum and olives.

2) More efficient methods of irrigation can be used. For example, drip irrigation delivers small volumes of water directly to crop roots (reducing the amount lost by evaporation).

Drip irrigation

3) These techniques reduce the demand on water supplies and make food production more reliable.

Increase water supplies

1) Reservoirs and wells can be built to increase water supplies.

2) These make more water available during a drought, reducing deaths from dehydration, reducing conflicts over supplies and making food production more reliable.

Reservoirs are man-made lakes that store water — they're created behind dams that are built across rivers.

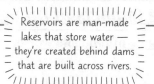

A rural well

Aid

Aid can help reduce the impacts of drought in more than one way:

- Emergency aid (like food and water tankers) can stop people dying from dehydration or starvation.

- Aid can be used to fund development projects, e.g. building wells or water pipes, to make more water available during droughts.

Some Strategies are More Sustainable Than Others

There's a definition of a sustainable strategy back on p. 53. You need to know a bit about the sustainability of strategies to reduce the impact of drought:

1) Most of the strategies are sustainable because they're effective and environmentally friendly. Building wells can deplete groundwater supplies, which means there's less water for people in the future, so sometimes they're not sustainable. Building reservoirs can reduce other people's water supply downriver. This means it's not sustainable as it doesn't meet the needs of people alive now.

2) As usual, some are more sustainable than others because they're more cost-effective, e.g. buying pipes for drip irrigation can be expensive, but it saves a lot of water and can be more cost-effective than emergency aid.

That's it, my humour supply is depleted — it wasn't even that full to begin with...

I hope this section has quenched your thirst for knowledge about climatic hazards because I've got nothing else to tell you. But hold on — the forecast for the next page has predicted a heavy downpour... of questions. I am hilarious.

Revision Summary for Section Six

Wow, another section down, you really are flying through this revision. Well, that's an assumption — if you've just opened up the book and randomly landed on this page then nice try, but you're not going any further until you can answer all of the questions below. You don't have to do them all in one go — that would be too much to ask, so just take your time. If you're finding it all a bit confusing then just flick back a few pages and jog your memory.

1) What is a climatic hazard?
2) What is a tropical storm?
3) Where do tropical storms develop?
4) Why do tropical storms lose strength over land?
5) How long do tropical storms usually last?
6) Describe two characteristics of the eyewall in a tropical storm.
7) Describe four primary impacts of tropical storms.
8) Describe four secondary impacts of tropical storms.
9) Give three reasons why the impacts of tropical storms are more severe in LEDCs.
10) Give two reasons why people continue to live in the areas where tropical storms happen.
11) Describe how tropical storms can be predicted.
12) Describe two ways buildings can be designed to withstand a tropical storm.
13) Why is it expensive to predict tropical storms?
14) a) Name an LEDC and an MEDC where a tropical storm or drought caused a disaster.
    b) Describe two primary impacts and two secondary impacts of each disaster.
    c) Explain why the severity of the impacts was different in the two places.
15) What is a drought?
16) Why are water supplies depleted during a drought?
17) Describe one climatic condition that causes droughts to happen.
18) Give one reason why people continue to live in the areas where droughts happen.
19) Describe two primary impacts of a drought.
20) Describe five secondary impacts of a drought.
21) How does overgrazing increase the impacts of droughts?
22) What are drought-resistant crops?
23) Describe one reason why the impacts of droughts are more severe in LEDCs.
24) Explain how efficient irrigation can reduce the impacts of droughts.
25) Give two examples of how people can conserve water at home to reduce the impacts of droughts.
26) a) Give two ways to increase water supplies.
    b) Why does increasing water supplies reduce the impacts of droughts?
27) Explain how aid can be used to help reduce the impacts of droughts.

Measuring Development

OK, this topic's a bit trickier than the other human ones, but fear not — I'll take it slowly.

Development is when a Country is Improving

1) When a country develops it basically gets better for the people living there — their quality of life improves (e.g. their wealth, health and safety). Some people think quality of life just includes wealth, but it doesn't. (When you're just on about wealth it's usually referred to as economic development.)

2) The level of development is different in different countries, e.g. France is more developed than Ethiopia.

3) Development is pretty hard to measure because it includes so many things. But you can compare the development of different countries using 'development indicators'. You need to know these ones:

TYPE	NAME	WHAT IT IS	A MEASURE OF...	AS A COUNTRY DEVELOPS IT GETS...
ECONOMIC	Gross Domestic Product (GDP)	The total value of goods and services a country produces in a year. It's often given in US dollars (US$).	Wealth	Higher ↑
ECONOMIC	GDP per capita	GDP divided by the total population (also called GDP per head).	Wealth	Higher ↑
SOCIAL	Birth rate	The number of live babies born per thousand of the population per year.	Female education and availability of birth control	Lower ↓
SOCIAL	Death rate	The number of deaths per thousand of the population per year.	Quality of and access to healthcare	Lower ↓
SOCIAL	Infant mortality rate	The number of babies who die under 1 year old, per thousand babies born.	Sanitation and healthcare	Lower ↓
SOCIAL	People per doctor	The average number of people for each doctor.	Access to healthcare	Lower ↓
SOCIAL	Literacy rate	The percentage of adults who can read and write.	Access to education	Higher ↑
SOCIAL	Access to safe water	The percentage of people that can get clean drinking water.	Sanitation	Higher ↑
SOCIAL	Life expectancy	The average age a person can expect to live to.	Quality of and access to healthcare	Higher ↑
SOCIAL	Physical Quality-of-Life Index (PQLI)	This is a number that's calculated using life expectancy, literacy rate and infant mortality rate.	Lots of things	Higher ↑
SOCIAL	Calorie intake	The average number of calories eaten per day.	Access to a healthy and varied diet	Higher ↑
OTHER	Human Development Index (HDI)	A number that's calculated using life expectancy, literacy rate, education level (e.g. degree) and income per head.	Lots of things	Higher ↑

Development Indicators have Some Disadvantages

1) Economic indicators can be inaccurate for countries where trade (the exchange of goods and services) is informal (not taxed). They're also affected by exchange rate changes (they're often given in US$).

2) Social indicators are more difficult to measure but they give a better indication of quality of life. Also, there aren't any indicators for important social factors like human rights.

3) The measures can be misleading when used on their own because they're averages — they don't show up elite groups in the population or variations within the country. Using more than one measure or using the HDI or PQLI (which combine loads of measures) avoids this problem.

Revision indicators — they're called exams...

...and talking of exams you'd better get learnin' the 12 development indicators listed above. Make sure you know what each one means and whether it gets higher or lower as a country develops. In fact, shut the book and test yourself now.

Categories of Development

Deciding how to <u>categorise different countries</u> based on <u>development</u> is about as <u>easy</u> as <u>licking your elbow</u>.

In The Past there was the First World, Second World and Third World...

1) In the <u>1960s</u>, countries were classified as <u>First World</u>, <u>Second World</u> or <u>Third World countries</u>.

2) The <u>First</u> World countries were <u>rich countries</u> with lots of <u>manufacturing</u> and <u>services</u>.
They included the USA, western Europe countries, Australia and Japan.

3) The <u>Second</u> World countries were <u>communist</u> countries with lots of <u>manufacturing</u>.
They included eastern European countries (e.g. Poland), the USSR (now Russia) and China.

4) All the <u>other</u> countries were classified as <u>Third</u> World countries.

5) But some people thought <u>ranking</u> countries like this was <u>disrespectful</u> to countries labelled Third World.

...then there were MEDCs and LEDCs...

1) From the <u>1980s</u> countries have been classified into <u>two</u> categories based on <u>how economically developed</u> they are.

2) <u>Richer</u> countries are classed as <u>More Economically Developed Countries</u> (MEDCs) and <u>poorer</u> countries are classed as <u>Less Economically Developed Countries</u> (LEDCs).

3) <u>MEDCs</u> are generally found in the <u>north</u>. They include the USA, European countries, Australia and New Zealand.

4) <u>LEDCs</u> are generally found in the <u>south</u>. They include India, China, Mexico, Brazil and all the African countries.

Brandt line   MEDCs   LEDCs

5) In the 1980s the <u>Brandt Report</u> was published. It discussed the <u>divide</u> of <u>rich countries</u> to the <u>north</u> and <u>poorer countries</u> to the <u>south</u>. The line used to show the <u>divide</u> is called the <u>Brandt line</u>.

6) But this simple classification <u>can't tell</u> you which countries are <u>developing quickly</u> and which <u>aren't really developing at all</u>. Also, the classifications are based on <u>wealth</u>, which <u>doesn't</u> always <u>match development level</u> — for example, literacy can be high even if GDP is low.

The different categories can overlap, e.g. China is an MEDC and an NIC.

...and Now there are Lots of Other Categories Too

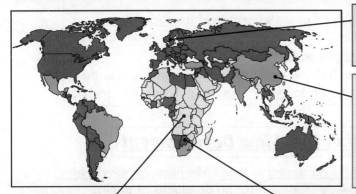

<u>Most developed countries</u> — these are the <u>most developed</u> countries in the world. For example, the UK, Norway, USA, Canada, France.

<u>Newly Industrialising Countries (NICs)</u> — these are <u>rapidly getting richer</u> as their <u>economy</u> is moving from being based on <u>primary industry</u> (e.g. agriculture) to <u>secondary industry</u> (manufacturing). For example, China, India, Brazil, Mexico, South Africa.

<u>Least developed countries</u> — these are the world's <u>poorest</u> countries with the <u>lowest quality of life</u>. For example, Ethiopia, Chad, Angola.

<u>Middle income countries</u> — these countries <u>aren't really poor</u>, but <u>aren't rich either</u> (they're kind of in the middle). They're <u>developing quickly</u>, but not as quickly as NICs are. For example, Albania, Bulgaria, Poland.

Tabby, moggy, feral — less useful cat-egories...

Unfortunately, revising development categories is a <u>teeny bit more difficult</u> now that there are lots of different <u>categories</u> (I wish those geographers would make their minds up about what to call things — sooooo inconsiderate).

Factors Affecting the Level of Development

Zzzzzz... oh, sorry, I nodded off for a minute there. You need to know the <u>reasons why</u> some countries are <u>less developed</u> and some are <u>more developed</u> (i.e. why they're at <u>different stages of development</u>).

Environmental Factors Affect How Developed a Country Is

A country is more likely to be <u>less</u> developed if it has...

1 A POOR CLIMATE

1) If a country has a poor climate (<u>really hot</u> or <u>really cold</u>) they <u>won't</u> be able to <u>grow much</u>.
2) This <u>reduces</u> the amount of <u>food produced</u>.
3) In some countries this can lead to <u>malnutrition</u>, e.g. in Chad and Ethiopia. People who are malnourished have a <u>low quality of life</u>.
4) People also have <u>fewer crops to sell</u>, so <u>less money</u> to <u>spend on goods and services</u>. This also <u>reduces</u> their <u>quality of life</u>.
5) The government gets <u>less money from taxes</u> (as less is sold and bought). This means there's <u>less to spend</u> on <u>developing the country</u>, e.g. to spend on <u>improving healthcare</u> and <u>education</u>.

2 POOR FARMING LAND

If the land in a country is <u>steep</u> or has <u>poor soil</u> (or no soil) then they <u>won't produce a lot of food</u>. This has the same effect as a poor climate (see above).

3 LIMITED WATER SUPPLIES

Some countries <u>don't have a lot</u> of <u>water</u>, e.g. Egypt, Jordan. This makes it <u>harder</u> for them to <u>produce a lot of food</u>. This has the same effect as a poor climate (see above).

4 LOTS of NATURAL HAZARDS

1) A natural hazard is an <u>event</u> that has the potential to <u>affect peoples' lives</u> or <u>property</u>, e.g. earthquakes, tsunamis, volcanic eruptions, tropical storms, droughts, floods.
2) When natural hazards <u>do affect</u> people's lives or property they're called <u>natural disasters</u>.
3) Countries that <u>have a lot of natural disasters</u> have to <u>spend a lot of money rebuilding</u> after disasters occur, e.g. Bangladesh.
4) So natural disasters <u>reduce quality of life</u> for the people affected, and they <u>reduce</u> the amount of <u>money</u> the government has to spend on <u>development projects</u>.

5 FEW RAW MATERIALS

1) Countries <u>without</u> many <u>raw materials</u> like <u>coal</u>, <u>oil</u> or <u>metal ores</u> tend to <u>make less money</u> because they've got <u>fewer products to sell</u>.
2) This means they have <u>less money</u> to <u>spend on development</u>.
3) Some countries <u>do</u> have a lot of raw materials but still <u>aren't very developed</u> because they don't have the <u>money</u> to <u>develop</u> the <u>infrastructure</u> to <u>exploit them</u> (e.g. roads and ports).

There are Three Main Political Factors that Slow Development

1) If a country has an <u>unstable government</u> it <u>might not invest</u> in things like <u>healthcare</u>, <u>education</u> and <u>improving the economy</u>. This leads to <u>slow development</u> (or no development at all).
2) Some <u>governments</u> are <u>corrupt</u>. This means that <u>some people</u> in the country <u>get richer</u> (by breaking the law) while the <u>others stay poor</u> and have a <u>low quality of life</u>.
3) If there's <u>war</u> in a country the <u>country loses money</u> that could be spent on development — <u>equipment</u> is <u>expensive</u>, <u>buildings</u> get <u>destroyed</u> and <u>fewer people work</u> (because they're fighting). War also directly <u>reduces</u> the <u>quality of life</u> of the people in the country.

Hot and dry — good for holidays, bad for development...

So, if a country is <u>rubbish for farming</u>, <u>floods</u> keep wrecking the place or it has a <u>dodgy government</u>, then it's going to be <u>less developed than others</u>. There are a <u>few exceptions</u> though, e.g. Japan gets battered by natural hazards but is developed.

Factors Affecting the Level of Development

Countries really do have a tough time trying to develop. It's not just things like earthquakes and a shortage of water that hold them back — things like <u>trade</u>, <u>debt</u> and <u>mucky water</u> are to blame too...

Economic Factors Affecting Development Include Trade and Debt

A country is more likely to be <u>less</u> developed if it has...

1 POOR TRADE LINKS

1) Trade is the <u>exchange</u> of <u>goods</u> and <u>services</u> <u>between countries</u>.

2) <u>World trade patterns</u> (who trades with who) seriously influence a country's <u>economy</u> and so affect their <u>level of development</u>.

3) If a country has <u>poor trade links</u> (it trades a small amount with only a few countries) it <u>won't make a lot of money</u>, so there'll be <u>less to spend on development</u>.

2 LOTS of DEBT

1) Very poor countries <u>borrow money</u> from <u>other countries</u> and <u>international organisations</u>, e.g. to help cope with the aftermath of a natural disaster.

2) This money has to be <u>paid back</u> (sometimes with <u>interest</u>).

3) Any <u>money</u> a country makes is <u>used to pay back</u> the money, so <u>isn't used to develop</u>.

3 AN ECONOMY BASED ON PRIMARY PRODUCTS

1) Countries that mostly trade <u>primary products</u> (raw materials like wood, metal and stone) tend to be <u>less developed</u>.

2) This is because you <u>don't make much profit</u> by selling primary products. Their <u>prices</u> also <u>fluctuate</u> — sometimes the <u>price falls below</u> the <u>cost of production</u>.

3) This means people <u>don't make much money</u>, so the government has <u>less to spend on development</u>.

4) Countries that trade <u>manufactured goods</u> tend to be <u>more developed</u>.

5) This is because you usually make a <u>decent profit</u> by selling manufactured goods. Wealthy countries can also <u>force down</u> the <u>price of raw materials</u> that they buy from poorer countries.

Social Factors Affect Development Too

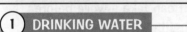

1 DRINKING WATER

1) A country will be <u>more developed</u> if it has <u>clean drinking water available</u>.

2) If the only water people can drink is <u>dirty</u> then they'll <u>get ill</u> — waterborne diseases include typhoid and cholera. <u>Being ill</u> a lot <u>reduces</u> a person's <u>quality of life</u>.

3) <u>Ill people can't work</u>, so they <u>don't add money to the economy</u>, and they also <u>cost money to treat</u>.

4) So if a country has unsafe drinking water they'll have <u>more ill people</u> and so <u>less money to develop</u>.

2 THE PLACE OF WOMEN IN SOCIETY

1) A country will be <u>more developed</u> if <u>women</u> have an <u>equal place with men in society</u>.

2) Women who have an equal place in society are more likely to be <u>educated</u> and to <u>work</u>.

3) Women who are educated and work have a <u>better quality of life</u>, and the country has <u>more money</u> to <u>spend on development</u> because there are <u>more people contributing</u> to the <u>economy</u>.

3 CHILD EDUCATION

1) The <u>more children</u> that <u>go to school</u> (rather than work) the <u>more developed</u> a country will be.

2) This is because they'll get a <u>better education</u> and so will get <u>better jobs</u>. Being educated and having a good job <u>improves</u> the person's <u>quality of life</u> and <u>increases</u> the <u>money</u> the country has to <u>spend on development</u>.

Debt — the cause of slow development and my lack of a fancy mobile phone...

Reading this page makes you realise <u>how nice</u> the <u>UK</u> is — there's trade galore, clean water and women work. Don't forget there are always <u>exceptions</u> to the rules above, e.g. countries that <u>export oil</u> (a primary product) are often <u>quite rich</u>.

Development and Aid

One way <u>less developed countries</u> are given a <u>helping hand</u> is through <u>international aid</u>.

Some Types of International Aid Speed Up Development

1) Aid is <u>given</u> by one country to another country in the form of <u>money</u> or <u>resources</u> (e.g. food, doctors).

2) The country that <u>gives</u> the aid is called the <u>donor</u> — the one that <u>gets</u> the aid is called the <u>recipient</u>.

3) There are <u>two</u> main <u>sources</u> of aid from donor countries — <u>governments</u> (paid for by <u>taxes</u>) and <u>Non-Governmental Organisations</u> (NGOs, paid for by <u>voluntary donations</u>).

4) There are <u>two</u> different ways <u>donor governments</u> can give aid to recipient countries:

> • <u>Directly</u> to the recipient — this is called <u>bilateral aid</u>.
>
> • <u>Indirectly</u> through an <u>international organisation</u> that distributes the aid — this is called <u>multilateral aid</u>.

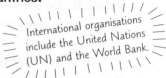

International organisations include the United Nations (UN) and the World Bank.

5) Bilateral aid can be <u>tied</u> — this means it's given with the <u>condition</u> that the <u>recipient country</u> has to <u>buy</u> the <u>goods and services</u> it needs <u>from</u> the <u>donor country</u>. This helps the <u>economy</u> of the donor country. However, if the goods and services are <u>expensive</u> in the donor country, the aid <u>doesn't go as far</u> as it would if the goods and services were bought <u>elsewhere</u>.

6) Aid can be classed as either <u>short-term</u> or <u>long-term</u> depending on <u>what it's used for</u>:

SHORT-TERM AID

1) This is money or resources that help recipient countries <u>cope</u> during <u>emergencies</u>, e.g. floods.

2) The aid has an <u>immediate impact</u> so <u>more people</u> will <u>survive</u> the emergency.

3) There are <u>disadvantages</u> though:
   • The <u>stage of development</u> of the recipient country remains <u>unchanged</u> overall.
   • If either country is <u>slow to react</u>, aid may not get to where it's <u>most needed</u>.
   • The aid <u>may not reach</u> those who <u>need it</u> because of things like <u>theft</u> and <u>transport problems</u>.

LONG-TERM AID

1) This is money or resources that help recipient countries to <u>develop</u>, e.g:
   • It's used to build <u>dams</u> and <u>wells</u> to <u>improve clean water supplies</u>.
   • It's used to construct <u>schools</u> to <u>improve literacy</u> rates.

2) Over time, recipient countries become <u>less reliant</u> on <u>foreign aid</u> as they become more developed.

3) However, it can <u>take a while</u> before the aid <u>benefits</u> a country, e.g. hospitals take a long time to build.

7) For both types of aid the <u>recipient</u> may become <u>dependent</u> on the aid — they <u>don't bother spending their own money developing themselves</u> because they get it from someone else.

8) In some recipient countries aid is <u>misused</u> because they have <u>corrupt governments</u> — the government uses the money and resources to <u>fund</u> their <u>lifestyle</u> or to pay for <u>political events</u>.

International Aid may not be Sustainable

1) To be <u>sustainable</u>, aid must help development in ways that <u>don't irreversibly damage</u> the <u>environment</u> or <u>use up resources</u> (including <u>money</u>) faster than they can be replaced.

2) An example of a <u>sustainable aid project</u> would be a scheme that helps people switch from earning money by <u>deforestation</u> to earning money in a <u>more environmentally friendly way</u>. This <u>reduces environmental damage</u> and makes sure <u>trees</u> are <u>still there for future generations</u>.

3) An example of an <u>unsustainable aid project</u> would be investment in <u>large</u>, <u>shallow water wells</u> in areas with <u>little rainfall</u>. Use of the wells could <u>use up water faster</u> than it's <u>replaced</u>. This would mean that the <u>amount of water</u> available for <u>future use</u> would be <u>reduced</u>.

Still or sparkling, minister?

Watching Live Aid on DVD doesn't count as revision...

Quite a bit to remember on this page. Make sure you know the different <u>types of aid</u> — it's not all the same, chaps. Why not try writing down the most recent aid appeals you saw on telly and listing what type of aid they were supplying.

Aid Project — Case Study

There are loads of aid projects going on around the world. Here's an example of one...

FARM-Africa helps the Development of Rural Africa

1) FARM-Africa is a non-governmental organisation (NGO) that provides aid to eastern Africa.
2) It's funded by voluntary donations.
3) It was founded in 1985 to reduce rural poverty.
4) FARM-Africa runs programmes in five African countries — Ethiopia, Sudan, Kenya, Uganda and Tanzania.
5) FARM-Africa has been operating in Ethiopia since 1988. Here are four of the projects it runs there:

Project	Region	Problem	What's being done	Helping...	Sustainability
Rural Women's Empowerment	Various	There are very few opportunities for Ethiopian women to make money. This means they have a low quality of life and struggle to afford things like healthcare.	Women are given training and livestock to start farming. Loan schemes have been set up to help women launch small businesses like bakeries and coffee shops. Women have been given legal training to advise other women of their rights.	Around 15 160 people.	Once the new businesses have been set up they'll continue to grow and make money. This means that money will be available as a future resource.
Prosopis Management	Afar	Prosopis, a plant introduced by the government to stabilise soils, has become a pest — it invades grazing land, making farming difficult.	Farmers are shown how to convert prosopis into animal feed. The animal feed is then sold, generating a new source of income.	Around 4400 households.	Once the farmers have been taught the new technique they'll be able to carry on using it. This means that money will be available as a future resource.
Community Development Project	Semu Robi	Frequent droughts make farming very difficult. This reduces the farmer's income and can lead to malnutrition. Semu Robi is a remote region, so getting veterinary care for livestock is difficult.	People are given loans to buy small water pumps to irrigate their farmland. This reduces the effects of drought. People are trained in basic veterinary care so they can help keep livestock healthy.	Around 4100 people.	The project means people are able to farm more crops and animals. This means they can earn more money. But if too much water is used there won't be any left for other people.
Sustainable Forest Management	Bale	Forests are cut down to make land for growing crops and grazing livestock. Trees are also cut down for firewood. This reduces resources for future generations.	Communities are taught how to produce honey and grow wild coffee. These are then sold, so people can make money without cutting down trees. Communities are also taught how to make fuel-efficient stoves that use less wood. This also reduces deforestation.	Around 7500 communities.	Less deforestation means there'll still be trees for future generations. Also, people can make money themselves by selling the coffee and honey.

You'd need a seriously meaty plough to farm the whole of Africa...

Yes, it's another case study for you. I think this one's pretty interesting though, and it's not too difficult to get your head around. Make sure you can describe the problems in Ethiopia as well as the aid projects that tackle them.

Revision Summary for Section Seven

So, if you've been paying attention for the last six pages your knowledge of development should have developed a lot. If your brain feels a little bit stretched, that's a good indicator of development. Another good indicator of development is this revision summary — have a bash through these questions to find out what you know.

1) What is Gross Domestic Product (GDP)?
2) Define birth rate.
3) Does literacy rate get higher or lower as a country develops?
4) What is the average age a person can expect to live to called?
5) Give three things that are used to calculate the PQLI for a country.
6) What is the name of the development indicator that's calculated using other indicators such as literacy rate and income per head?
7) Give one disadvantage of economic development indicators.
8) A single measure of development could be used to figure out how developed a country is. What is the disadvantage of this?
9) What does MEDC stand for?
10) Describe the global distribution of MEDCs and LEDCs.
11) What problems are associated with using only MEDC and LEDC to classify countries?
12) Describe what a Newly Industrialising Country is and give one example.
13) Give one example of a middle income country.
14) Give one way a poor climate affects a country's development.
15) Is a country likely to be more or less developed if it doesn't have a lot of water?
16) How do natural hazards affect a country's development?
17) Describe a political factor that affects a country's development.
18) How do poor trade links affect a country's development?
19) Explain why countries that mostly trade primary products are less developed.
20) Why are countries with unsafe drinking water more likely to be less developed?
21) Explain why a country is more developed if women have an equal place with men in society.
22) Is a country more or less developed if more children are at school rather than at work?
23) What is multilateral aid?
24) a) What is tied aid?
    b) Give one disadvantage of tied aid.
25) What's the difference between short-term and long-term aid?
26) Give one advantage of short-term aid.
27) Give one disadvantage of aid.
28) a) Name an aid project in an LEDC that you have studied.
    b) Describe how the aid project is improving quality of life for the people in the area.
    c) Comment on how sustainable the aid project is.

Types of Industry and Employment Structure

Industry and economic development are linked — but unfortunately, first you need to know what the types of industry are, where they are, why they're there... the list goes on.

There are Four Different Types of Industry

The four types are — primary, secondary, tertiary and quaternary. The employment structure of a country describes what proportion of its workforce is employed in each type of industry.

1) Primary industry involves collecting raw materials, e.g. farming, fishing, mining and forestry.

2) Secondary industry involves turning a product into another product (manufacturing), e.g. making textiles, furniture, chemicals, steel and cars.

3) Tertiary industry involves providing a service — anything from financial services, nursing and retail to the police force and transport.

4) Quaternary industry is high technology — where scientists and researchers investigate and develop new products, e.g. in the electronics and IT industry.

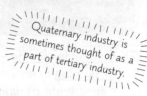
Quaternary industry is sometimes thought of as a part of tertiary industry.

A Country's Employment Structure Changes as it Develops

LEDCs

1) Most of the workforce is employed in primary industry.

2) Few people work in secondary industry because there's not enough money to invest in the technology needed for this type of industry, e.g. to build large factories.

3) A small percentage of people work in tertiary industry — usually in cities where there are banks, hospitals and schools.

4) There's no quaternary industry because the country doesn't have enough educated or skilled workers, and it can't afford to invest in the technology needed, e.g telescopes.

Many workers in LEDCs don't appear in official statistics because they work in jobs that aren't taxed or monitored by the government, e.g. street traders. These jobs are referred to as the informal sector of the economy.

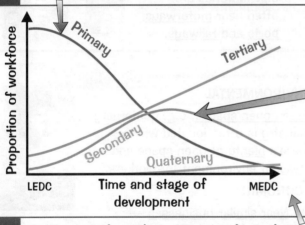

Proportion of workforce

Primary

Tertiary

Secondary

Quaternary

LEDC — Time and stage of development — MEDC

NICs are countries where the employment in secondary industry is increasing. As a country becomes more developed the percentage of people employed in secondary industry increases then decreases. This is because as infrastructure develops, businesses move their factories to LEDCs where labour is cheaper.

MEDCs

1) Few people work in primary industry because machines replace workers, and it's cheaper to import primary products from other countries, e.g. farm workers in LEDCs earn very little so the produce is cheap.

2) Fewer people work in secondary industry than in NICs (see above).

3) Most people work in tertiary industry because there's a skilled and educated workforce, and there's a high demand for services like banks and shops.

4) There's some quaternary industry because the country has lots of highly skilled labour and has money to invest in the technology needed.

Employment structure changes over time because countries become more wealthy, and education and infrastructure improve.

Primary industry — making small chairs, glitter and crayons...

There's a close link between a country's wealth and its employment structure. Primary industry doesn't make much profit whereas quaternary industry can make a lot. And more profit means a more economically developed country.

Location of Industry

Economic activity or industry doesn't just happen anywhere, you know. A sweet shop in the middle of nowhere wouldn't get much business — it needs to be close to all those sticky-fingered sweet-eaters.

Many Factors Influence the Location of Industry

PRIMARY INDUSTRY

ENVIRONMENTAL

1) Lots of raw materials, e.g. fisheries are by the coast.

2) A suitable climate — this affects the type of farming in an area, e.g. potatoes need a temperate climate and bananas need a tropical climate.

3) Good quality soil — farming will be most successful where there's nutrient-rich soil.

ECONOMIC

1) Cheap land, e.g. farming uses large areas of land so it's found where land is cheap.

2) Good transport routes, e.g. quarries need roads or railways to transport rock.

SECONDARY INDUSTRY

ENVIRONMENTAL

1) Close to raw materials, e.g. paper factories are often located near forests.

2) Plenty of flat land — it's easier to build a factory where the land is flat.

3) A local water supply — industries that use a lot of water are often located near rivers.

ECONOMIC

1) A suitable local market, e.g. bakers are often based in residential areas.

The 'market' means where the people are that buy the product.

2) Government grants, e.g. grants or loans may be provided to encourage industries to locate in particular areas.

3) Lots of workers, e.g. factories need lots of staff.

4) Good transport routes, e.g. factories are often near motorways, ports and railways.

Well hello...

TERTIARY INDUSTRY

ENVIRONMENTAL

Green open spaces, e.g. schools are often in areas that provide a pleasant environment for pupils.

ECONOMIC

1) A suitable local market, e.g. you get lots of shops in cities as there are plenty of customers.

2) Good transport routes, e.g. shops are located near public transport routes so customers can get to them easily.

3) Skilled and educated workers, e.g. hospitals are often located near universities where there are skilled workers available.

SOCIAL

Enough local people to support the service, e.g. schools are found where there are lots of children.

QUATERNARY INDUSTRY

ENVIRONMENTAL

Green open spaces, e.g. quaternary industry is often located where there's plenty of open space and a pleasant environment for workers.

ECONOMIC

1) Near similar businesses — research and development companies often cluster together (e.g. on a science park) so that information and ideas can be shared.

2) Skilled and educated workers, e.g. scientific research companies are often near universities.

SOCIAL

Lots of nice quality housing, e.g. good houses nearby will encourage workers to move there.

It'd be nice to have a biscuit factory round here...

Bit of a complicated page, this — industry is all about location, location, location. And because it's complicated you need to make extra sure you know it. Use the old drill — cover this page and scribble down as much as you can.

Location of Industry in an LEDC — Case Study

If you're not feeling very industrious, I think I can help you. A case study on why industry locates where it does should boost your enthusiasm — then you can turn this raw material into some exam fodder.

The Location of Industry in an LEDC — Kenya

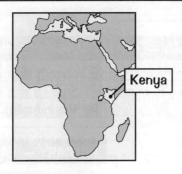

Kenya

TERTIARY — TOURISM

There's a strong tourist industry in the Rift Valley. The area has several National Parks and lakes (e.g. Lake Turkana and Lake Magadi).

TERTIARY — TOURISM

There's a strong tourist industry near Mount Kenya because it's the second highest mountain in Africa and has a National Park.

SECONDARY — MANUFACTURING

There are lots of manufacturers in Nairobi that produce textiles, foods and drinks. The area has good transport links (including an airport) and a good labour supply — Nairobi's population is about 3 million people.

PRIMARY — FARMING

Livestock (e.g. camels and cattle) are reared on farms in the North Eastern Province because the climate is too dry for crops, but is suitable for grazing.

PRIMARY — FARMING

There are lots of farms in the Nyanza and Western Provinces that produce coffee, tea, tobacco and fruits — these are the areas that receive enough rainfall to grow crops.

SECONDARY — MANUFACTURING

There are cement works in the Coast Province because they use limestone from the nearby deposits as a raw material.

TERTIARY — TOURISM

There's a strong tourist industry in the Coast Province because of its beaches, e.g. Diani Beach.

PRIMARY — MINING

There's a large mine in Magadi that extracts trona (a mineral that's used to make glass). The mineral forms around Lake Magadi as the water evaporates.

Camilla the camel was fed up of case studies — she had the hump...

...and who can blame her. Look on the bright side though, the good news is that Kenya is an LEDC so it doesn't have any quaternary industry. That means there's only three different types of industry to remember for this page.

Location of Industry in an MEDC — Case Study

You also need to know why <u>industry locates</u> where it does in MEDCs. Well, you're in the right place to find out, 'cos here's a case study of <u>what's where</u> and <u>why</u> in the good ol' UK.

The Location of Industry in an MEDC — the UK

QUATERNARY — ELECTRONICS

Many <u>electronics companies</u> are based in the <u>Central Lowlands of Scotland</u> because of the <u>local skilled labour supply</u> — nearby <u>universities</u> such as Glasgow, Edinburgh and Heriot-Watt provide <u>electronics</u> and <u>engineering graduates</u>.

SECONDARY — CHEMICAL PROCESSING

There are <u>chemicals works</u> in <u>North East England</u> because they're near to <u>offshore oil rigs</u> that provide the <u>raw material</u> for the industry.

TERTIARY — TOURISM

There's a strong <u>tourist industry</u> in <u>Cumbria</u> because of the <u>beautiful scenery</u>.

PRIMARY — FARMING

There are lots of <u>farms</u> in <u>Lincolnshire</u> and <u>East Anglia</u> because of the <u>good soil</u> and <u>mild climate</u>. It's also very <u>flat</u>, which makes it easier to use <u>large machinery</u> such as tractors.

SECONDARY — MANUFACTURING

<u>Government grants</u> have encouraged <u>car manufacturers</u> to locate in <u>Merseyside</u>, e.g. in 1998 <u>Jaguar cars</u> began production at the <u>Halewood plant</u> after receiving a <u>£50 million grant</u> from the <u>Government</u>.

QUATERNARY — HIGH TECHNOLOGY

There are many <u>high technology industries</u> near <u>Cambridge</u> because the <u>university</u> provides <u>educated</u> and <u>skilled workers</u>.

PRIMARY — MINING

<u>Coal mining has been a major industry</u> in <u>Nottinghamshire</u> since the 13th century because of the <u>coalfields</u> in the area. Although <u>most mines</u> have now <u>closed</u>, a small amount of mining still goes on.

TERTIARY — RETAIL

There are lots of <u>shops</u> in <u>London</u> because there are <u>plenty of customers</u> and <u>good public transport</u>. There are also excellent <u>transport links</u> for the <u>delivery</u> of <u>products</u> to shops.

QUATERNARY — HIGH TECHNOLOGY

There are many <u>high technology industries</u> along the <u>M4 corridor</u> (the area near the M4 motorway). The area is close to <u>universities</u> (Bristol, Oxford and Reading) that provide <u>skilled workers</u>, and the motorway is good for <u>communication</u>.

Case studies and London buses — you wait for ages and two come along at once...

So if you like a touch of farming, the east of England's the place to be. <u>Industry</u> within your <u>local town</u> will be based in <u>suitable places</u> for <u>similar reasons</u>. Try listing some local companies and working out why they might be based there.

Location of Industry Over Time

Time changes everything, honest. It even changes where industry locates — and not just from the revision chair to the exam room. To help you keep up with all the changes, I've made a table.

The Location of Industry Changes Over Time

The location of industry changes with time due to environmental, economic and social reasons:

	ENVIRONMENTAL	ECONOMIC	SOCIAL
Primary Industry	• Raw materials become exhausted so industry moves elsewhere, e.g. quarries move once all the rock has been extracted. • Climate change means that some crops can be grown in new areas, e.g. increasing temperatures mean that vineyards have been set up in Kent.	• Lower costs make previously expensive areas cheaper, e.g. improvements in oil drilling technology mean that it's now economically viable (worth it) to reach much deeper oilfields.	• Improved transport routes mean that primary industry can be located in more remote areas, e.g. better roads in Brazil mean forestry is possible in new parts of the Amazon rainforest. • Government policies change to allow industry in new areas, e.g. in 2008, Western Australia lifted its ban on uranium mining.
Secondary Industry	• New energy sources mean that industry doesn't have to be close to power sources, e.g. in the past many factories used coal for power so were near coalfields, but now they use electricity from the National Grid.	• Changing capital (money) investment patterns encourage industry to locate to new areas, e.g. the UK Government and private investment in manufacturing in Scotland is encouraging industries to locate there.	• Government policies change, which encourages industries to settle in different locations, e.g. the UK Government gives incentives to companies to open factories (and create jobs) in deprived areas. • Improved transport facilities mean more people have access to cars or public transport so can travel further to work, e.g. in the past many factories were located in city centres so workers could get there easily.
Tertiary Industry	• Workers increasingly want a nice working environment with pleasant surroundings, so industry moves in order to attract workers, e.g. offices move from the centre of a city to the outskirts. • Extreme environments are becoming more popular for tourists as travel gets cheaper and easier, e.g. the tourist industry is developing in Antarctica.	• Changing capital investment patterns encourage industry to locate to new areas, e.g. the UK Government has provided the money to build a new hospital development in Manchester and new mental health facilities in Merseyside.	• Improved transport facilities mean retailers don't have to be located in city centres for their customers to reach them, e.g. most people have access to cars now so there are more out-of-town shopping centres. • Shopping patterns have changed so people don't just shop on their local high street, e.g. many retailers sell products over the internet, so they don't need to be near their customers.
Quaternary Industry	• Workers increasingly want to work in a nice environment with pleasant surroundings, so industry moves in order to attract them, e.g. research centres are often outside cities. • Some scientific research industries have environmental needs, e.g. research into GM crops needs land to grow experimental crops away from ordinary crops.	• Changing capital investment patterns encourage industry to locate to new areas, e.g. increasing investment in digital telecommunications in rural areas encourages businesses to move there.	• The labour force moves as training and housing changes, e.g. electronics industries often locate near universities that have good electronics courses.

Any minute now the joke factory will move to my office...

...and then I'll be able to write something hilarious. While you're waiting, cover up this page and see how much of this table you can scribble down. Then, if you check back in a few minutes I may have something witty for you as a reward.

Environmental Impacts of Industry

As you might have guessed now we're 78 pages into the book, geographers are <u>obsessed</u> by <u>impacts</u>.

Primary Industries *Have a Huge Impact on the Environment*

FARMING

1) <u>Monoculture</u> (growing just <u>one</u> type of crop) <u>reduces biodiversity</u> as there are <u>fewer habitats</u>.

2) <u>Removing hedgerows</u> to increase the area of farmland <u>destroys habitats</u>. It also <u>increases soil erosion</u> (hedgerows normally act as windbreaks).

3) <u>Herbicides</u> can <u>kill wildflowers</u>, <u>pesticides</u> can <u>kill other insects</u> (as well as pests) and <u>fertilisers</u> can <u>pollute rivers</u>, <u>killing fish</u> (this is called <u>eutrophication</u>).

4) <u>Making fertilisers</u>, <u>pesticides</u> and <u>herbicides</u> uses <u>fossil fuels</u>, which <u>adds</u> to <u>global warming</u>.

5) <u>Cows produce methane</u>, which also <u>adds</u> to <u>global warming</u>.

Biodiversity is the number and variety of organisms. A habitat is where an organism lives.

There's loads more about global warming on pages 81-83.

MINING

1) Mining <u>destroys large areas</u> of <u>land</u>, so there are <u>fewer habitats</u> and <u>food sources</u> for animals and birds. This <u>reduces biodiversity</u>.

2) Mining <u>uses lots of water</u>, so it can <u>deplete water sources</u>.

3) Some kinds of mining can cause <u>water pollution</u>.

FISHING

1) Overfishing <u>depletes resources</u> and <u>upsets food chains</u>.

2) Fishing boats can <u>leak oil</u> and <u>diesel</u>, which <u>kills aquatic animals</u>.

FORESTRY

1) <u>Fewer trees</u> means <u>fewer habitats</u> and <u>food sources</u> for animals and birds. This <u>reduces biodiversity</u>.

2) <u>Soil erosion</u> is more common as there are <u>fewer trees</u> to <u>hold</u> the <u>soil together</u>.

3) Trees <u>remove CO_2</u> from the <u>atmosphere</u> when they <u>photosynthesise</u>, so without them <u>less</u> CO_2 is removed. <u>More forestry</u> means <u>more</u> CO_2 in the <u>atmosphere</u>, which adds to <u>global warming</u>.

4) Without trees, <u>less water is removed</u> from the <u>soil</u> and <u>evaporated</u> into the atmosphere. So <u>fewer clouds form</u> and <u>rainfall</u> in the area is <u>reduced</u>. Reduced rainfall <u>reduces plant growth</u>.

Secondary Industries *Cause Pollution*

1) <u>Factories</u> can cause <u>land</u>, <u>air</u> and <u>water pollution</u>, e.g. <u>dyes</u> from <u>textile</u> factories can <u>pollute rivers</u> and <u>sulfur dioxide</u> emissions from <u>metal works</u> can cause <u>acid rain</u>.

2) <u>Habitats</u> are <u>destroyed</u> if factories are <u>built</u> in the <u>countryside</u>.

3) Some factories use a <u>huge amount of energy</u>, e.g. ice cream factories. This energy usually comes from <u>burning fossil fuels</u>, so <u>adds</u> to <u>global warming</u>.

Tertiary *and Quaternary Industries Use a Lot of Energy*

1) <u>Tertiary and quaternary</u> industries <u>use a lot of energy</u>, e.g. to run <u>computers</u>, <u>shops</u> or <u>vehicles</u>.

2) This energy usually comes from <u>burning fossil fuels</u>, so <u>adds</u> to <u>global warming</u>.

3) Also, all the <u>resources</u> these industries <u>use</u> cause an <u>impact</u> when they're <u>manufactured</u>. E.g. <u>trees</u> are <u>cut down</u> and made into <u>paper</u> in <u>factories</u>.

Maybe I'll turn my computer off standby then...

Crikey, <u>industry</u> has a <u>lot of environmental impacts</u> (even more impacts than I have skateboarding bruises). Make sure you <u>learn them</u> so you can trot them out in <u>neat handwriting</u> for the examiner (if it's illegible you won't get any marks).

Development and Environmental Impacts

Industry is good for a country's pocket (it helps its economy to develop), but it's not great for its back garden. Fear not though my friend, there are things that can be done to make the garden a beautiful oasis.

Economic Development often Damages the Environment

1) An increase in industry in an area helps it to develop economically — it creates more jobs, which increases the wealth of the area and the local people.

2) But some industries damage the environment a lot.

3) This means there's conflict between economic development (by increasing industry) and protecting the environment.

4) Economic development can aim to be sustainable though. To be sustainable it has to increase the wealth of an area in a way that doesn't stop people in the future getting what they need. Basically this means not depleting resources or damaging the environment irreversibly.

There are Ways to Make Economic Development More Sustainable

Economic development can be more sustainable if the industries that cause it reduce their environmental impacts. For example:

FARMING

1) Use fewer herbicides, pesticides and fertilisers (although this reduces crop yield).

2) Maintain hedgerows instead of removing them.

MINING

1) Laws can be introduced to help reduce water pollution.

2) The habitats in a quarry can be restored once it's disused, e.g. by planting trees and creating ponds.

FORESTRY

Laws can be introduced that make logging companies plant one tree for each one cut down. This means that there will still be trees for the future. It also reduces soil erosion.

FISHING

1) Quotas (limits on the number of fish caught) can be introduced to stop overfishing.

2) Fish can be raised on fish farms to prevent wild stocks from running out.

FACTORIES

1) Laws to reduce water, air and land pollution can be introduced.

2) Building on brownfield sites (derelict areas that have been used, but aren't being used any more) stops habitat destruction.

3) Energy use can be reduced by using more energy efficient devices.

OFFICES, SHOPS and VEHICLES

1) Turning off computers instead of leaving them on standby reduces energy use.

2) Using more efficient vehicles reduces the amount of fossil fuel burnt.

I have an ongoing conflict with my brother about chips...

He thinks ketchup is the sauce of choice for chips. But I (correctly) believe mayonnaise is far superior. However, on fish fingers (made from sustainably farmed stocks), there's no such conflict. It's ketchup all the way. Obviously.

Development and Environmental Impacts — Case Study

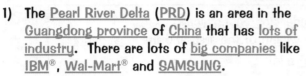

Oooh — case study time. Excellent.

Manufacturing is Helping Economic Development in South China

1) The Pearl River Delta (PRD) is an area in the Guangdong province of China that has lots of industry. There are lots of big companies like IBM®, Wal-Mart® and SAMSUNG.

2) The industries increase economic development by increasing the wealth of the area. In 1980 the area had a GDP of US$8 billion and by 2001 it had grown to about US$100 billion.

3) Industry has created lots of jobs in the area. E.g. Dongguan has over 25 000 factories and Honda employs over 6000 people in Guangzhou and Zhongshan.

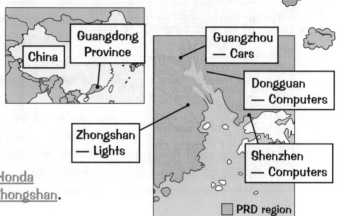

But There are Environmental Impacts

1) There's so much air pollution that the area's often covered in smog. Lots of it comes from power plants that burn coal. For example, the levels of sulfur dioxide and nitrogen dioxide in the air in the PRD area are around two to three times higher than in other areas of the Guangdong province. These gases cause acid rain.

2) Pollution from factory waste and untreated sewage also means that the water quality of the area is very poor. For example, Pearl River water in Guangzhou is only suitable for farm use (not for drinking or domestic use).

3) Humans aren't the only ones suffering from the pollution — it's affecting wildlife habitats too. The Pearl River drains into the South China Sea so this area is also affected. Local species such as the Chinese white dolphin are becoming endangered as a result.

Management Strategies Aim to Reduce the Impacts

The environmental impacts of industry in the PRD are being managed in several ways. For example:

> The Pearl River Delta Air Quality Management Plan aims to reduce the amount of air pollution by 2010. They're trying to reduce the amount of sulfur dioxide emitted from power plants by 40% compared to 1997 levels. One way to do this is to reduce the dependence on coal for energy production by using natural gas instead, which produces fewer toxic emissions.

> The Government has pledged about US$7.1 billion to help clean up the Pearl River. It's being used to build around 30 sewage works and water treatment facilities — these will reduce the amount of untreated domestic sewage and industrial waste that goes into the river.

These management strategies are sustainable because they aim to reduce air and water pollution without stopping industry from expanding or closing down factories. This means that people will still be able to live and work in the PRD in the future as there will still be jobs and resources like water for them to use.

Dongguan — wasn't that one of the three musketeers...

Phew, hope all the smog round here hasn't clogged your brain. Maybe your holiday job in the local salad factory isn't so bad after all — at least there's some nice coleslaw-scented air to breathe. Although that might not be your thing.

Global Climate Change — Causes

Pretty much <u>every type of industry</u> adds to <u>global warming</u> in some way or another.
That's pretty bad, but what's even worse is you have to know ALL about it.

Global Warming *is* a Type of Climate Change

1) <u>Climate change</u> is any <u>change</u> in the <u>weather</u> of an area over a <u>long period</u>.

2) <u>Global warming</u> is the <u>increase</u> in <u>global temperature</u> over the <u>last century</u>.

3) So global warming is a <u>type</u> of climate change.

4) Annoyingly, global warming also <u>causes other types</u> of climate change, e.g. <u>decreased rainfall</u> in some places.

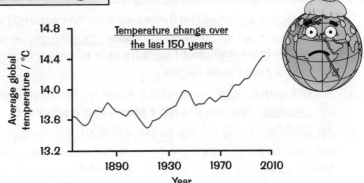

Temperature change over the last 150 years

Average global temperature / °C — Year (1890, 1930, 1970, 2010)

An Increase *in* Greenhouse Gases *is* Causing Global Warming

1) The <u>temperature</u> of the Earth is a <u>balance</u> between the heat it <u>gets</u> from the <u>Sun</u> and the heat it <u>loses</u> to <u>space</u>.

2) <u>Gases</u> in the <u>atmosphere</u> naturally act like an <u>insulating layer</u> — they <u>trap outgoing heat</u>, helping to keep the Earth at the right temperature. This is called the <u>greenhouse effect</u> ('cos it's a bit like a greenhouse trapping heat).

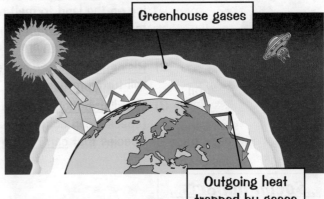

Greenhouse gases

Outgoing heat trapped by gases

3) Gases that trap heat are called <u>greenhouse gases</u> — they include <u>carbon dioxide</u> (CO_2) and <u>methane</u> (CH_4).

4) Human activities like <u>farming</u>, <u>forestry</u> and <u>manufacturing</u> have <u>increased</u> the <u>concentration of carbon dioxide</u> and <u>methane</u> in the atmosphere (see p. 78). For example, CO_2 has gone up from <u>280 ppm</u> (parts per million) in <u>1850</u> to around <u>380 ppm today</u>.

Thicker layer of greenhouse gases

More outgoing heat trapped by gases causes the Earth to warm up

5) There's a <u>scientific consensus</u> (general agreement) that the <u>increase in greenhouse gases</u> (caused by human activity) has <u>caused global warming</u> by making the <u>greenhouse effect stronger</u>.

Which climate shall I change into today — the hot or the cold one...

Global warming isn't as confusing as you first think — it's just like <u>humans</u> are <u>adding</u> an <u>extra-snuggly duvet</u> around the world. The only thing is the Earth was happy enough with <u>just one</u> duvet and now it's getting a <u>bit sweaty</u>. Eugh.

Global Climate Change — Impacts

Climate change won't just mean you can wear a bikini in Scotland — it's got a bucketful of other impacts.

Climate Change will have Economic Impacts...

1) Climate change will affect farming in different ways around the world:

- In higher latitudes (further away from the equator) warmer weather will mean some farmers can make more money — some crop yields will be increased, and they'll be able to grow new types of crops to sell, e.g. olives in the UK.
- In lower latitudes (nearer the equator) farmers' income may decrease because it's too hot and dry for farming.

2) Climate change means the weather is getting more extreme. This means more money will have to be spent on predicting extreme weather events (like floods and tropical storms). More money will also have to be spent reducing their impacts and rebuilding after them.

3) Industries that help to reduce the effects of climate change will become bigger and make more money.

Don't forget — global warming is a type of climate change.

...Environmental Impacts...

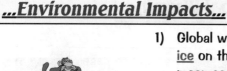

1) Global warming is causing sea level to rise — increasing temperature causes ice on the land to melt and water in the oceans to expand. Sea level rise will mean some habitats will be lost as low-lying coastal areas are submerged, e.g. the Maldives are a low-lying group of islands at risk from sea level rise.

2) Rising temperature and decreased rainfall will mean some environments will turn into deserts.

3) The distribution of some species may change due to climate change (species can only live in the areas where the conditions suit them best). Species that can't move may die out.

...Social Impacts...

1) People won't be able to grow as much food in lower latitudes (see above). This could lead to malnutrition, ill health and death from starvation, e.g. in places like central Africa.

2) More people will die because of more extreme weather events.

3) Hotter weather makes it easier for some infectious diseases to spread, e.g. malaria could become common in the UK. This will lead to more ill health and more deaths from disease.

4) Some areas will become so hot and dry that they're uninhabitable. Also, some places will be flooded by the rising sea. So people will have to move, which could lead to overcrowding in other areas.

...and Political Impacts... phew

1) Water will become more scarce in some places. Competition over water could lead to war between countries.

2) Climate change may cause people to move (see above). This means some countries will have to cope with increased immigration and emigration.

3) Governments are under pressure to come up with ways to slow climate change or reduce its effects.

Olives in the garden and warmer weather — bring on global warming...

They're always banging on about climate change and global warming in the news, which is exactly why you need to learn their impacts — examiners love hot topics (they're a bit weird like that — I love chocolate, shoes and palaeontology).

Global Climate Change — Responses

Most of the <u>responses</u> to climate change are pretty boring to be honest — they involve <u>cutting emissions</u> of <u>greenhouse gases</u>. This can be done <u>globally</u>, <u>nationally</u> and <u>locally</u>, so everyone gets a slice of the fun.

The Kyoto Protocol was a Global Response

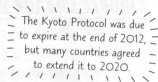

The Kyoto Protocol was due to expire at the end of 2012, but many countries agreed to extend it to 2020.

From 1997, <u>most countries</u> in the world agreed to <u>monitor</u> and <u>cut greenhouse gas emissions</u> by signing an <u>international agreement</u> called the <u>Kyoto Protocol</u>:

1) The aim was to <u>reduce global</u> greenhouse gas emissions by <u>5% below 1990 levels</u> by <u>2012</u>.

2) Each country was set a <u>target</u>, e.g. the <u>UK</u> agreed to reduce emissions by <u>12.5%</u> by 2012.

3) Another part of the protocol was the <u>carbon credits trading scheme</u>:

- <u>Countries</u> that came <u>under</u> their emissions target got <u>carbon credits</u> which they could <u>sell</u> to countries that <u>didn't meet</u> their emissions target. This meant there was a <u>reward</u> for having <u>low emissions</u>.

- <u>Countries</u> could also <u>earn</u> carbon credits by helping <u>poorer countries</u> to <u>reduce</u> their emissions. The idea was that poorer countries would be able to reduce their emissions <u>more quickly</u>.

4) <u>Not all countries</u> agreed to the Kyoto Protocol though — the <u>USA</u> didn't agree, and they have the <u>highest emissions</u> of any country in the world (<u>22%</u> of global CO_2 emissions in 2004).

There are also National and Local Responses to Climate Change

NATIONAL RESPONSES

1) **TRANSPORT STRATEGIES**
<u>Governments</u> can <u>improve public transport networks</u> like buses and trains. For example, they can make them run <u>faster</u> or <u>cover</u> a <u>wider area</u>. This <u>encourages more people</u> to <u>use public transport</u> instead of cars, so CO_2 emissions are <u>reduced</u>.

2) **TAXATION**
Governments can <u>increase taxes</u> on cars with <u>high emissions</u>, e.g. in the UK there are <u>higher tax rates</u> for cars with <u>higher emissions</u>. This <u>encourages</u> people to <u>buy cars</u> with <u>low emissions</u>, so emissions are <u>reduced</u>.

LOCAL RESPONSES

1) **CONGESTION CHARGING**
<u>Local authorities</u> can <u>charge</u> people for <u>driving cars</u> into <u>cities</u> during <u>busy periods</u>, e.g. there's a congestion charge to drive into <u>central London</u> during busy times of the day. This <u>encourages</u> people to use their cars <u>less</u>, which <u>reduces emissions</u>.

2) **RECYCLING**
- Local authorities can <u>recycle more waste</u> by building <u>recycling plants</u> and giving people <u>recycling bins</u>. Recycling materials means <u>less energy is used</u> <u>making new materials</u>, so emissions are <u>reduced</u>.

- Local authorities can also <u>create energy</u> by <u>burning recycled waste</u>, e.g. Sheffield uses a waste incinerator to supply 140 buildings with energy.

3) **CONSERVING ENERGY**
- Local authorities give <u>money</u> and <u>advice</u> to make homes <u>more energy</u> efficient, e.g. by doing things like <u>improving insulation</u>. This means people <u>use less energy</u> to <u>heat</u> their homes, because <u>less</u> is <u>lost</u>. Emissions are <u>reduced</u> because <u>less energy</u> needs to be <u>produced</u>.

- <u>Individuals</u> can also conserve energy by doing things like <u>switching lights off</u> and <u>not</u> leaving electric gadgets on <u>standby</u>.

My response to climate change — slap on the suncream and bust out the shades...

Climate change is a <u>global problem</u>, so the response to deal with it needs to be on a <u>global scale</u>. That means <u>everyone</u> has to do their bit, from world leaders down to folk like us. Now, did I leave my hair straighteners on...

Revision Summary for Section Eight

At last, the end of another long, hard section — well nearly the end. Before you stop for a well-earned cup of tea and an episode of Hollyoaks, there's just the small matter of this list of questions.
It's really in your best interests to have a look through them, because if there are any you can't answer then you can bet your favourite pair of pants that that's exactly what will come up in the exam.

1) What is meant by the employment structure of a country?

2) Define what primary industry is and give an example.

3) Define what secondary industry is and give an example.

4) How does the employment structure of a country change as it becomes more developed?

5) Give one environmental and one economic factor that influences where secondary industry is located.

6) Give one environmental and one economic factor that influences where quaternary industry is located.

7) a) Name an LEDC you have studied and give four examples of industries found there.

   b) Explain why each of those industries is located where it is.

8) a) Name an MEDC you have studied and give four examples of industries found in that country.

   b) Explain why each of those industries is located where it is.

9) Give one environmental, one economic and one social reason why the location of primary industry changes over time.

10) Give two environmental impacts of these primary industries:

   a) Farming

   b) Mining

   c) Fishing

   d) Forestry

11) How do secondary industries affect the environment?

12) How do tertiary and quaternary industries affect the environment?

13) Explain why there's often conflict between economic development and protecting the environment.

14) Give two ways to make primary industry more sustainable.

15) Give two ways to make secondary industry more sustainable.

16) Give two ways to make tertiary and quaternary industry more sustainable.

17) a) For an area you have studied describe how industry has contributed to economic development there.

   b) What have the environmental impacts of the industry been?

   c) What is being done in the area to reduce the impacts?

18) What is global warming?

19) What is causing global warming?

20) Give two economic, two environmental, two social and two political impacts of climate change.

21) How did the Kyoto Protocol aim to reduce the impact of climate change?

22) Describe one national and one local response to climate change.

Globalisation Basics

Globalisation is a long word and a big topic. Better get started then...

Globalisation *is the Process of Countries Becoming More Integrated*

1) Every country has its own political and economic systems as well as its own culture.

2) Globalisation is the process of all the world's systems and cultures becoming more integrated — it's the whole world coming together like a single community.

3) It happens because of international trade (the production and sale of goods), international investment and improvements in communications.

Improvements *in Communications* have *Increased Globalisation*

Improvements in ICT (Information and Communication Technology) and transport have increased globalisation by increasing trade and investment:

ICT

1) Improvements in ICT include e-mail, the internet, mobile phones and phone lines that can carry more information and faster.

2) This has made it quicker and easier for businesses all over the world to communicate with each other. For example, a company can have its headquarters in one country and easily communicate with branches in other countries. No time is lost so it's really efficient.

Transport

1) Improvements in transport include more airports, high-speed trains and larger ships.

2) This has made it quicker and easier for people all over the world to communicate with each other face to face.

3) It's also made it easier for companies to get supplies from all over the world, and to distribute their product all over the world. They don't have to be located near to their suppliers or their product market anymore.

Multinational Companies (MNCs) *also Increase Globalisation*

1) MNCs are companies that produce products, sell products or are located in more than one country. For example, Sony is a MNC — it manufactures electronic products in China and Japan, and sells many of them in Europe and the USA.

2) MNCs are usually very rich companies that employ lots of people and have a large output (they make loads of products every year). For example:

> Ford is an American-owned MNC that makes cars. In 2008, it produced over 5 million cars worldwide. It also employs over 200 000 people at about 90 different sites around the world.

3) MNCs increase globalisation by linking together countries through the production and sale of goods.

4) They also bring the culture from their country of origin to many different countries, e.g. McDonald's brings Western-style fast food to other countries.

Globalisation is going large — with extra barbecue sauce...

Globalisation is a bit of a weird concept so don't panic if you don't get it straight away. Learn how improvements in ICT and transport have increased globalisation, and don't forget about MNCs — they're very important, as you'll see next...

Multinational Companies (MNCs)

I'm very <u>globalised</u>, me — I get my clothes from Calcutta, my bananas from Brazil, and my microwave from Mexico... via the <u>MNC</u> at the end of my road (cleverly disguised as a supermarket).

MNCs Affect Economic Development

1) MNCs <u>create jobs</u> in an area. This <u>increases</u> the <u>wealth</u> of the <u>area</u> (due to <u>taxes</u>) and the wealth of the <u>local people</u> (due to <u>employment</u>).

2) Taxes are used to <u>improve infrastructure</u> (e.g. <u>roads</u>) and <u>services</u> (e.g. <u>schools</u>, <u>hospitals</u>, etc.). People also have <u>more money to spend</u>. Both of these things <u>attract more businesses</u> to the area (including more MNCs), creating <u>even more jobs</u>, and so on...

3) This <u>cycle</u> (more jobs, leading to more services, leading to more jobs...) is called the <u>multiplier effect</u>.

4) MNC <u>factories</u> are often <u>located in LEDCs</u> because <u>labour is cheaper</u>, which means they make <u>more profit</u>. (<u>Less strict health and safety regulations</u> make it <u>cheaper</u> too.)

5) They also locate in LEDCs because <u>working hours</u> are <u>longer</u>, so <u>products can be made quicker</u>.

6) MNC <u>headquarters</u> and <u>research centres</u> are usually located in <u>MEDCs</u> because there are <u>more skilled and educated people</u> (but there are <u>some MNC factories</u> in MEDCs as well).

MNCs have Positive Effects...

MNCs can have a <u>positive effect</u> on the areas where they <u>locate</u>:

1) MNCs <u>create jobs</u> where they're located. This can lead to <u>more jobs</u> through the <u>multiplier effect</u>.

2) When they locate to LEDCs they create some <u>skilled jobs</u>, e.g. jobs in factory offices. This <u>encourages more education</u> and <u>training</u> in the area, as they can lead to a better job.

3) Workers can get <u>higher wages</u> and <u>more reliable incomes</u> compared to other jobs, e.g. farming.

4) MNCs <u>spend money</u> on <u>infrastructure</u> (e.g. airports and roads) and <u>pay taxes</u> that are used to <u>develop</u> the <u>economy</u> and country.

5) <u>Local companies</u> <u>supply</u> the MNCs, <u>increasing</u> their <u>income</u>.

<u>Positive effects</u> of MNCs <u>outside</u> of where they <u>locate</u> include <u>lower priced goods</u> and a <u>wider range</u> of goods available.

...and Negative Effects

MNC Inc. Head Office

The only real negative is the massive shoes we have to wear. They're ridiculous.

1) The <u>jobs</u> created <u>aren't always secure</u> — the MNC could <u>relocate</u> at any time.

2) Employees in <u>LEDCs</u> may have to work <u>long hours</u> in <u>poor conditions</u>.

3) Employees in <u>LEDCs</u> may be paid <u>lower wages</u> than employees in <u>MEDCs</u>.

4) <u>Other local companies</u> may <u>struggle</u> to <u>find business</u> or <u>workers</u>, so <u>shut down</u>.

5) <u>Profits</u> go <u>back</u> to the country the MNC is originally from (usually an <u>MEDC</u>).

6) <u>Large sites</u> will attract <u>lots of traffic</u>, which <u>increases pollution</u> in the area.

7) Sites also <u>produce pollution and waste</u>, which is bad for the <u>environment</u> and for <u>people's health</u>.

The big <u>negative effect</u> of MNCs <u>outside</u> of where they <u>locate</u> is <u>increased greenhouse gas emissions</u> caused by <u>transporting raw materials</u> and <u>finished products</u> all over the place. This <u>adds to global warming</u> (see p. 81 for more).

MNCs are everywhere — and I mean everywhere...

Geography types are always making up <u>long names</u> for things (multinational companies), then <u>squishing</u> them down to <u>just a few letters</u> (MNCs). I don't know what they get out of it, but it seems to keep them happy.

MNCs — Case Study

FACT: only cockroaches and case studies can survive a direct nuclear explosion.

Wal-Mart® is a Retail MNC with Headquarters in the USA

1) Wal-Mart began in 1962 when Sam Walton opened the first store in Arkansas, USA.

2) More stores opened across Arkansas, then across the USA, and more recently across the world, e.g. in Mexico, Argentina, China, Japan, Brazil, Canada and the UK (where it's called ASDA).

3) Wal-Mart sells a variety of products, e.g. food, clothes and electrical goods.

4) Wal-Mart is the biggest retailer in the world — it owns over 8000 stores and employs over 2 million people.

WALL MART

£55.99 £55.99 £48.99

Bricking it since 1962

Wal-Mart has Positive Effects...

1) Wal-Mart creates lots of jobs in different countries, e.g. in construction, manufacturing and retail services. E.g. in Mexico, Wal-Mart employs over 150 000 people and in Argentina, three new stores opened in 2008, creating nearly 450 jobs.

2) Local companies and farmers supply goods to Wal-Mart, increasing their business. E.g. in Canada, Wal-Mart works with over 6000 Canadian suppliers, creating around US$11 billion of business for them each year.

■ = Location of Wal-Mart stores

3) Wal-Mart offers more skilled jobs in LEDCs. E.g. all the Wal-Mart stores in China, are managed by local people.

5) The company invests money in sustainable development. E.g. in Puerto Rico, 23 Wal-Mart stores are having solar panels fitted on their roofs to generate electricity.

4) Wal-Mart donates hundreds of millions of dollars to improve things like health and the environment in countries where it's based. E.g. in 2008 in Argentina, Wal-Mart donated US$77 000 to local projects and gave food and money to help feed nearly 12 000 poor people.

...and Negative Effects

1) Some companies that supply Wal-Mart have long working hours. E.g. Beximco in Bangladesh supplies clothing. Bangladesh has a maximum 60 hour working week, but some people claim employees at Beximco regularly work 80 hours a week.

2) Not all Wal-Mart workers are paid the same wages. E.g. factory workers in the USA earn around $6 an hour, but factory workers in China earn less than $1 an hour (although this is quite a lot in China).

3) Some studies have suggested that Wal-Mart stores can cause smaller shops in the area to shut — they can't compete with the low prices and range of products on sale.

4) The stores are often very large and out-of-town, which can cause environmental problems. Building them takes up large areas of land and people driving to them causes traffic and pollution. For example, the largest Wal-Mart store is in Hawaii and it covers over 27 000 m² — that's over three times the size of the football pitch at Wembley Stadium.

Wal-Mart — for all your walling needs...

If you know squillions of details for another MNC case study then that's fine (as long as you do know them — owning some of their products doesn't count). If you don't then get your memorising hat on (mine's a pink fez) and get learnin'.

The Impacts of Globalisation

Globalisation is on the increase, which can have some serious impacts on the whole world. Just think of a world where there's an ASDA, McDonald's and Starbucks in every town and city... oh, right.

Globalisation has Economic Impacts...

MEDCs

Globalisation has caused deindustrialisation in MEDCs — secondary manufacturing industries have moved to LEDCs (and NICs, see p. 67) because labour is cheaper. MEDCs have developed their tertiary and quaternary industries instead. This has increased the gap between rich and poor people:

> People who have good qualifications can find work in these well-paid industries. But poorer, unskilled workers struggle to find work because there are fewer manufacturing jobs.

LEDCs and NICs

Globalisation has caused industrialisation in LEDCs and NICs — secondary manufacturing industries have moved to LEDCs and NICs, e.g. China. But this can increase the gap between rich and poor in these countries too:

> MNCs create jobs, which has brought wealth to some people. But the wealth isn't spread evenly — a few people become wealthy, while many remain poor.

...Environmental Impacts...

1) Carbon emissions — transporting raw materials and products around the world increases the amount of carbon dioxide released. This adds to global warming (see p. 81).

2) Waste — people have access to more products at low prices, so they can afford to be more wasteful. Lots of waste ends up as landfill if it's not recycled.

3) Deforestation — increased global trade has meant countries in tropical areas can make money by growing crops to sell for profit (cash crops), e.g. oilseed plantations for alternative fuel. They clear forests to make space for crops. This destroys habitats, reducing biodiversity, and increases soil erosion.

4) Oil pollution — the more products that are transported around the world by ship, the more oil pollution there'll be. Oil pollution kills fish and seabirds.

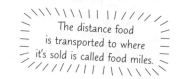
The distance food is transported to where it's sold is called food miles.

...and Social and Cultural Impacts

Globalisation can help to improve people's quality of life, particularly in LEDCs:

> Increased trade brings more jobs and money into the country. The government uses the money to improve infrastructure and services like healthcare and education. People have more money and access to lower priced goods. So they can afford more food, clothes and items like TVs.

But there are cultural impacts too. Some people think countries are losing their cultural heritage as we all listen to the same music, wear the same clothes and drive the same cars. But other people think globalisation's a good thing as it exposes people to other cultures.

Hit me, señora, one more time

MNCs make the world go round, the world go round, the world go round...

I bet you're within about a metre of something that was made in an exotic LEDC (or NIC) like Taiwan, Indonesia or China. Unless, like me, you're reading this on the loo, then you're near products made by happy little labrador puppies.

Revision Summary for Section Nine

I'll admit it... that wasn't the most thrilling of sections (for drama and excitement give me volcanoes any day of the week) — but I am excited about the whole world coming together as one big community. I'm sure we'll all get on famously. Anyway, before you put all this behind you and move on to something more uplifting, check you're a great big know-it-all with this useful bunch of bananas. I mean questions. Sorry.

1) What is globalisation?

2) How have improvements in ICT increased globalisation?

3) How have improvements in transport increased globalisation?

4) What is a MNC?

5) How do MNCs increase globalisation?

6) Describe the multiplier effect.

7) Give one reason why MNC factories are often located in LEDCs.

8) Why are MNC headquarters and research centres usually located in MEDCs?

9) a) Give two positive and two negative effects of MNCs on the areas they locate in.

   b) Give one positive and one negative effect of MNCs on areas outside of where they locate.

10) a) Name an MNC you have studied.

    b) Name two countries it is located in.

    c) Give two positive effects of the MNC.

    d) Give two negative effects of the MNC.

11) Describe the economic impact of globalisation on MEDCs.

12) How can globalisation increase the gap between rich and poor in LEDCs and NICs?

13) List three environmental impacts of globalisation.

14) Explain how globalisation can improve people's standard of living.

15) a) Describe a negative cultural impact of globalisation.

    b) Give a positive cultural impact of globalisation.

Geographical Enquiry

Geographical Enquiry — Overview

Alas, the Geographical Enquiry isn't when you enquire if you'll be finished with this book any time soon.

The Enquiry Involves Answering a Geographical Question

1) Geography is about where things happen, and explaining how and why they happen, e.g. where coastal erosion occurs, and how and why it happens.

2) Geographers ask a question, collect some data, analyse the data collected and use the results to answer the original question. And you get to do all this yourself during the Geographical Enquiry.

3) It's worth 60 marks in total (that's 25% of your final mark).

4) You just have to do one fieldwork focus task from a choice of four. You have to collect primary data (data you collect during fieldwork), analyse it and produce a written report all about it.

5) You'll get 16 hours of class time to analyse your data and write the report. Your report should be no more than 2000 words. Here's a flow chart to show you what to do:

> A hypothesis is a statement that you can investigate to see if it's true or false, e.g. 'rural-urban migration is caused by a shortage of services in rural communities'.

1. Pick a task and make up a question or hypothesis.

Pick one task from the tasks set by the exam board — these will be based on the themes of Rivers, Coasts, Population, Settlement and Economic Development. Ask your teacher if you're unsure which task you're completing. Then you need to ask a question or form a hypothesis that's relevant to your task. E.g. task — what are the characteristics of retail service provision in your local area? Hypothesis — the type of goods sold in shops changes as you move away from the centre of Bristelton, OR question — does the type of goods shops sell in Bristelton change as you move away from the centre?

2. Set the scene.

a) Introduce the task and your question or hypothesis, and explain how it links to the specification (the Key Theme it's based on, e.g. Rivers).

b) Describe and explain the results you're expecting.

c) Introduce the location of your study and any relevant geographical processes or concepts.

Page 91

3. Describe your methodology.

Describe the fieldwork methods you used, why you used them and explain any problems you had.

Page 91

4. Present and analyse your data.

Present your fieldwork data using graphs, tables, etc. Describe and explain what the data shows.

Page 92 to 93

5. Draw a conclusion and evaluate your investigation.

a) Draw a conclusion — use your data to answer your original question or say whether it supports your hypothesis or not.

b) Discuss whether the investigation was successful or not and what the limitations were.

c) Explain how you could improve and extend your study.

Page 93 to 94

Hippos like wallowing — my hippo-thesis...

Ask your teacher for a copy of the mark scheme — it says what your report should contain and how to get top marks.

Fieldwork Focus — Introduction and Methodology

Now you've got a general idea what the fieldwork focus involves, let's get down to the details. There's nowhere better to start than <u>preparation</u>, in fact here's some preparation I prepared earlier... (boom boom)

Good Preparation will Help You Later On

Here are a few of the things you could do <u>before starting</u> the fieldwork focus:

Research the area you're investigating —

Collect <u>background information</u> on the area you're studying (e.g. photos and maps). Study the <u>processes</u> or <u>concepts</u> that gave the area its <u>geographical features</u>.

Plan your fieldwork —

Plan your <u>methods</u> and what <u>equipment</u> you'll need. Think about <u>how much</u> data to collect — generally the <u>more</u> you collect the <u>more reliable</u> your <u>results</u> will be. Also think about how much <u>time</u> it'll take and <u>where</u> to collect data. And don't forget about <u>health and safety</u>.

Collect secondary data —

The fieldwork focus is mostly about <u>primary data</u> but you can use <u>relevant secondary data</u>. Look at <u>newspapers</u>, <u>books</u> and <u>websites</u>. Keep a <u>record</u> of <u>where</u> the data comes from for your <u>bibliography</u>.

You can also ask your <u>teacher</u> for <u>advice</u> on things like your <u>question</u>, <u>techniques</u> and <u>report layout</u>.

Setting the Scene is Your Introduction

1) <u>Introduce</u> the <u>task</u> and the <u>question</u> or <u>hypothesis</u> you're investigating. <u>Explain how</u> it links to the <u>Key Theme</u>. For example, investigating <u>local retail services</u> relates to the <u>Population and Settlement</u> Key Theme — the <u>types</u> of retail services you get change <u>within settlements</u>. You could investigate <u>what shops</u> you get <u>where</u> and <u>why</u>.

2) Introduce the <u>study area</u> and its <u>location</u> in detail and <u>explain why</u> you're investigating <u>that area</u>. Include things like <u>annotated photos</u> and <u>maps</u> with <u>titles</u>, <u>grid references</u>, <u>scales</u> and <u>keys</u>. <u>Mark on</u> the maps and photos <u>where</u> you <u>collected data</u>.

3) <u>Describe</u> and <u>explain</u> the <u>geographical processes and concepts</u> you're investigating — use this book to help. E.g. if you're looking at <u>rural-urban migration</u> explain <u>push and pull factors</u>.

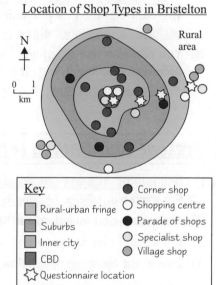

Location of Shop Types in Bristelton

Describe and Justify the Techniques You Used in The Methodology

You need to <u>describe</u> all the data collection methods you used, what they <u>involved</u>, <u>justify why</u> you used them and describe any <u>problems</u> you had. One way of showing this information is in a <u>table</u>:

Method	Description	Size	Where and when	Why	Problems
Questionnaire	Describe the method, e.g. say what you did and refer them to the blank questionnaire you've included.	Say how many questions were asked, how many people you asked and at what sites.	Describe where you asked people the questions (refer to any maps that show where) and when you asked them (time, day and date).	Explain why you chose a questionnaire and why you chose those questions, locations and numbers of people.	Explain any problems you encountered, e.g. very few people were willing to answer a questionnaire.

You can also draw diagrams to show how you used equipment.

There's method to my madness — you can read all about it in my table...

You don't need to use a <u>table</u> to describe and explain your methods. It's just a handy way to do it that means you shouldn't miss anything out — if you did miss anything, there'd be an <u>empty box</u>, which you'd notice. Super.

Fieldwork Focus — Data Presentation

You've made it to the fun part now — processing and presenting your data. It's graphs galore. And as it's geography, I'd bet my good arm (left if you're asking) that there'll be some colouring-in too.

You May Need to Process Some of Your Data

Now you've got lots of primary data lying around, you need to process it:

1) Data processing can mean organising data to make it easier to analyse and understand. E.g. it's no good putting every questionnaire answered in your report, it'd be too long and hard to analyse. Instead, you could make a table that gives a summary of the answers. Don't forget to include a copy of the blank questionnaire though, so you can refer to the questions you asked:

Q1	What type of goods are you buying today?
Q2	How far have you travelled to get here?
Q3	How did you get here today?

Question 1 answers:

Location	Electrical Goods	Clothes	Food	Books, CDs and DVDs	Other
CBD Shopping Centre	9	20	5	10	6
Village Shops	0	0	35	1	14

2) You can gain marks by manipulating your data before you present it too, e.g. you could calculate percentages, or averages (means and modes). The data can then be presented in a way that's easier to understand, e.g. a pie chart.

3) You can also use equations to manipulate your data before presenting it, e.g. the discharge of a river = cross-sectional area × average velocity.

Question 3 answers:

CBD Shopping Centre: 32%, 31%, 4%, 20%, 13%
Village Shop: 26%, 4%, 24%, 46%

Key
■ Bus
□ Car
□ Tram
□ Train
■ Walk

Present Your Data in Lots of Different Ways

1) Use lots of different presentation techniques in your report.
   For example, tables, pie charts, graphs, diagrams, maps, annotated sketches and photographs.

2) Make sure you include clear titles, scales, units and keys in your data presentation.

3) It's a good idea to use a computer to present at least one set of data, e.g. make a graph in Excel®.

4) Check out the examples below and pages 99-102 for other ways of presenting data:

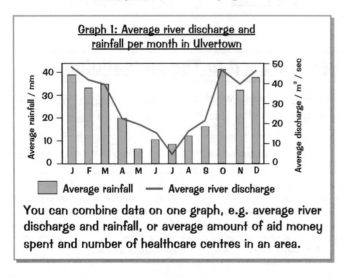

Graph 1: Average river discharge and rainfall per month in Ulvertown

You can combine data on one graph, e.g. average river discharge and rainfall, or average amount of aid money spent and number of healthcare centres in an area.

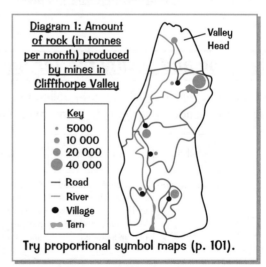

Diagram 1: Amount of rock (in tonnes per month) produced by mines in Cliffthorpe Valley

Valley Head

Key
· 5000
● 10 000
● 20 000
● 40 000
— Road
— River
● Village
▬ Tarn

Try proportional symbol maps (p. 101).

Data presentation — I find wrapping paper and a pretty bow help...

There are loads of different ways to present your data so don't just stick in bar charts and tables. Try some new and exciting techniques like choropleth maps or flow line maps — look at page 102 if you don't know what they are.

Fieldwork Focus — Analysis and Conclusions

Now we're onto the slightly trickier parts — analysis and conclusions. I've analysed my results and come to the conclusion that 9 out of 10 geographers prefer fieldwork to a good film and a bucket of popcorn.

Analysis is Describing and Explaining the Results

For more on correlations, see page 100.

1) Describe what your data shows — describe any patterns and correlations, and look for any anomalies (odd results). Make comparisons between different sets of data, use specific points from your data and reference what graph, table etc. you're talking about.

2) Explain what your data shows — explain why there are patterns and why different data sets are linked together. Use your geographical background information to help you and remember to use geographical terms.

For example:

Only 10% of people who visited Victoria shopping centre in the CBD of Bristelton were shopping for food items (see Table 1). This could be because the centre has relatively few food shops (three out of 50) and these only sell high order food items such as luxury chocolates (see Table 2). However, 70% of people who visited the shops in Gedling Village in the rural area outside Bristelton, were shopping for food items (see Table 1). This was the most popular reason for visiting these shops. Of the four shops in Gedling, three are village shops that mainly sell food and other low order goods. The fourth shop is a car showroom, which accounted for the high percentage of people (28%) visiting to buy other goods in the village (see Table 1).

GEDLING USED MOTORS

SOLD

A Conclusion Explains What You Found Out

Be careful when drawing conclusions. Some results show a link or correlation, but that doesn't mean that one thing causes another.

A conclusion is a summary of what you found out in relation to your original question or hypothesis. You need to:

1) Write a summary of your results — look at all your data and describe generally what it shows.

2) If you're investigating a question — give an answer to the question and explain why. If you're investigating a hypothesis — say whether your data supports the hypothesis or not and explain why.

3) Explain how your conclusion fits into the wider geographical world — think about how your conclusion and results could be used by other people or in further investigations.

For example:

I believe that my results support my original hypothesis that the type of goods sold by shops in Bristelton changes as you move away from the centre. The results of my survey showed that in general the type of goods sold by shops (either low or high order goods) was linked to the area of the city the shops were located in. For example, shops in the CBD sold mainly clothes and other high order goods, but shops in villages sold food and other low order goods. The results of the questionnaire suggest this is true because most people came to the CBD to buy high order goods and went to local village shops for low order food items...

I think my investigation would be useful for other people, e.g. people planning new retail developments in Bristelton. They could use my results to see what shops are already in the area, what goods are most commonly sold and how far people will travel to buy them.

You vill answer all my questions — ve have vays of making you talk...

You get marks for punctuation, grammar and spelling, so make sure you've checked all these. If it's word processed you can use the spellchecker. Don't forget to include plenty of geographical terms where you can too.

Fieldwork Focus — Evaluation

The last part of the fieldwork focus is <u>evaluating</u> what you did — saying what was good about it and what wasn't so great. And no, just putting you were brilliant and the investigation had no faults won't cut it.

The Evaluation is about How Successful the Investigation Was

Evaluation is all about <u>self assessment</u> — looking back at how <u>good or bad</u> your study was. You need to:

1) Identify any <u>problems</u> (<u>limitations</u>) with the <u>methods</u> you used and suggest how they could be <u>improved</u>. Think about things like:

> - The <u>size</u> of your <u>data sets</u> (bigger data sets are normally better).
> - If any <u>bias</u> slipped in (anything that might have made your results <u>unfair</u>, e.g. if you measured river velocity straight after a storm, or only interviewed people aged over 65).
> - Whether <u>other methods</u> would have been <u>more appropriate</u> or <u>more effective</u>.

2) Describe how <u>accurate</u> your results are and <u>link</u> this to the methods you used — say whether any <u>errors</u> in the methods affected the results.

3) Describe how <u>successful</u> your investigation was by commenting on the <u>validity</u> of your <u>conclusion</u>. You need to talk about how <u>problems</u> with the methods and the <u>accuracy</u> of the results affect the <u>validity</u> of the conclusion. Problems with methods lead to <u>less</u> reliable and accurate results, which affects the validity of the conclusion.

> - <u>Accurate</u> results are <u>as near</u> as possible to the <u>true answer</u> — they have <u>few errors</u>.
> - <u>Reliable</u> means that data can be <u>reproduced</u>.
> - <u>Valid</u> means that the data <u>answers</u> the <u>original question</u> and is <u>reliable</u>.

4) Make <u>suggestions</u> for how the study or methods could be <u>improved and extended</u> — think about what you <u>would have done</u> if you'd <u>had more time</u>.

For example:

> I believe my investigation was a <u>success</u> as the results <u>supported</u> my original hypothesis. However, the questionnaire was carried out on a <u>Saturday</u> when there was a <u>football</u> match on. This may have affected the <u>results</u> as <u>fewer people</u> that regularly come into Bristelton were consulted.
>
> As a result, my conclusion that shops in the CBD have the largest <u>sphere of influence</u> may be <u>less reliable</u>. The people I questioned may have <u>travelled a long way</u> for the football, so this would have affected the <u>average distance travelled</u>. I could improve this by carrying out the <u>same questionnaire</u> when there's no football match on, producing <u>more accurate and reliable</u> results and so a more <u>valid conclusion</u>.

This page is accurate, reliable and valid...

You're nearly done with <u>fieldwork focusing</u> now — all that remains is to check you've done everything. As luck would have it, there's a splendid <u>checklist</u> on the next page for that very purpose. I know, I think of everything.

Fieldwork Focus — Checklist

Last page on the fieldwork focus, yippe-ky-yay. And if you've done your job properly, this page should be a doddle — all you need to do is read this lovely checklist and make sure you can tick all the boxes.

Check You've Included Everything with this Handy Checklist

Tick the box once you've done each thing:

1)	Introduced your question or hypothesis and explained how it links to the specification.	☐
2)	Introduced the study area in detail.	☐
3)	Described the geographical processes or concepts.	☐
4)	Described what you did, when, where and why, and any problems for each method.	☐
5)	Processed your data and included many different presentation techniques (using a computer for some of them).	☐
6)	Included titles, keys, scales and units when presenting data. The diagrams have been numbered so you can refer to them.	☐
7)	Described and explained what your data shows.	☐
8)	Given a summary of your results in your conclusion.	☐
9)	Checked your conclusion answers your original question or supports your hypothesis.	☐
10)	Explained if your investigation has been a success.	☐
11)	Identified any problems with your methods.	☐
12)	Described any possible improvements and extensions.	☐
13)	Described whether the conclusion is valid.	☐
14)	Included a title page, contents table or page, page numbers and bibliography.	☐
15)	Checked your spelling, punctuation and grammar.	☐
16)	Used geographical terms.	☐

Present for the wonderful people at CGP for making this book — check...

And that my friends (as they say in show business) is that. OK, so no one says that in show business, but someone, somewhere, says it. Anyway, you've made it to the end of the section, well done. Feel free to feel smug.

Answering Questions

This section is filled with lots of lovely <u>techniques</u> and <u>skills</u> that you need for your <u>exams</u>. It's no good learning the <u>content</u> of this book if you don't know the skills you need to pass your exams too. First up, answering questions properly...

Make Sure you Read the Question Properly

It's dead easy to <u>misread</u> the question and spend five minutes writing about the <u>wrong thing</u>. Five simple tips can help you <u>avoid</u> this:

1) Figure out if it's a <u>case study question</u> — handily, these questions usually start '<u>Case Study</u>', but sometimes they're a bit <u>sneaky</u> and say things like '<u>refer to specific examples</u>'.

2) <u>Underline</u> the <u>command words</u> in the question (the ones that tell you <u>what to do</u>):

Answers to questions with 'explain' in them often include the word '<u>because</u>' (or '<u>due to</u>').

When writing about differences, '<u>whereas</u>' is a good word to use in your answers, e.g. 'the Richter scale measures the energy released by an earthquake whereas the Mercalli scale measures the effects'.

Command word	Means write about...
Describe	what it's <u>like</u>
Explain	<u>why</u> it's like that (i.e. give <u>reasons</u>)
Compare	the <u>similarities</u> AND <u>differences</u>
Contrast	the <u>differences</u>
Suggest	give <u>reasons</u> for

If a question asks you to describe a <u>pattern</u> (e.g. from a map or graph), make sure you identify the <u>general pattern</u>, then refer to any <u>anomalies</u> (things that <u>don't</u> fit the general pattern).

E.g. to answer 'describe the global distribution of volcanoes', first say that they're mostly on plate margins, <u>then</u> mention that a few aren't (e.g. in Hawaii).

3) <u>Underline</u> the <u>key words</u> (the ones that tell you what it's <u>about</u>), e.g. volcanoes, erosion, migration, central business district, population pyramid.

4) If the question says '<u>Use evidence from</u> Fig. 2...' you need to <u>refer</u> to the figure <u>in your answer</u>, e.g. quote numbers from it to back up your points.

5) <u>Re-read</u> the <u>question</u> and your <u>answer</u> when you've <u>finished</u>, just to check that what you've written really does <u>answer</u> the question being asked. A common mistake is to <u>miss a bit out</u> — like when questions say 'use <u>data</u> from the graph in your answer' or 'use <u>evidence</u> from the map'.

Case Study Questions are Level Marked

Case study questions are worth <u>9 marks</u>. They're <u>level marked</u>, which means you need to do these <u>things</u> to get the <u>top level</u> (3) and a <u>high mark</u>:

1) <u>Read</u> the question properly and figure out a <u>structure</u> before you start. Your answer needs to be well <u>organised</u> and <u>structured</u>, and written in a <u>logical</u> way.

2) Include plenty of <u>relevant details</u>:

- This includes things like <u>names</u>, <u>dates</u>, <u>statistics</u>, names of <u>organisations</u> or <u>companies</u>.
- Don't forget that they need to be <u>relevant</u> though — it's no good including the exact number of people killed in a flood when the question is about the <u>causes</u> of a flood.

3) Each of the <u>case study questions</u> also has another <u>3 marks</u> available for <u>spelling</u>, <u>punctuation</u> and <u>grammar</u>. To get <u>top marks</u> you need to:

- Make sure your <u>spelling</u>, <u>punctuation</u> and <u>grammar</u> is <u>consistently correct</u>.
- Write in a way that makes it <u>clear</u> what you mean.
- Use a <u>wide range</u> of <u>geographical terms</u> (e.g. destructive margin, backwash) <u>correctly</u>.

Describe the similarities and differences between compare and contrast...

The <u>differences</u> between the meanings of the command words are quite <u>subtle</u> — learn them so you get it right.

Labelling and Comparing

These next few pages give you some advice on what to do for specific types of questions.
Some of these skills will be helpful for your geographical enquiry too (see pages 90-95).

You Might have to Label Photos, Diagrams or Maps

If you're asked to label something:

1) Figure out from the question what the labels should do, e.g. describe the effects of an earthquake, label the characteristics of a waterfall, describe the coastal defences, etc.

2) Add at least as many labels as there are marks.

3) When describing the features talk about things like the size, shape and relief.
   Make sure you use the correct geographical names of any features, e.g. interlocking spur, meander.

Q: Label the characteristics of this coastline.

A:

Stack formed from a collapsed arch.

Arch caused by wave erosion (hydraulic action and corrasion).

Some vegetation on top of the cliffs.

Cave

Cracks and weaknesses in the rock making it susceptible to erosion.

Sandstone cliffs, easily eroded.

Look at Shapes When You Compare Plans and Photos

You might be given two items, like a plan and an aerial photograph, and be asked to use them together to answer some questions. Plans and aerial photos are a bit like maps — they show places from above.
Here are some tips for questions that use plans and photos:

1) The plan and photo might not be the same way up.

2) Work out how the photo matches the plan — look for the main features on the plan like a lake, a big road or something with an interesting shape, and find them on the photo.

3) Look at what's different between the plan and the photo and think about why it might be different.

Q: Look at the development plan for Crystal Bay (2000) and the photo taken after development in 2009.

   a) Name the area labelled A in the photo.

   b) Give one difference you can see between the photo and the plan.

A: a) Madeleine Park.

   b) The roads have been built in slightly different areas.
      There's a small harbour area in front of the apartments.

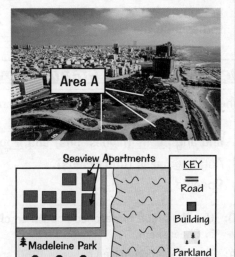

Area A

Seaview Apartments

Madeleine Park

KEY
Road
Building
Parkland
Sea

It isn't only fashionistas that are interested in labels...

You might have to use plans or photos in your exams to answer all sorts of questions — take your time and read the question carefully so you know exactly what you should be doing. Up next maps and graphs, whoop whoop.

Describing Maps and Graphs

One thing we geographers know how to do well is colouring in <u>maps</u> and <u>graphs</u>. You might get maps and graphs in the exams, but you'll probably have to <u>describe what they show</u>, rather than break out the crayons.

Describing Distributions <u>on Maps</u> — <u>Describe the Pattern</u>

1) In your exams you could get questions like, 'use the map to <u>describe</u> the <u>distribution</u> of volcanoes' and '<u>explain</u> the <u>distribution</u> of factories'.

2) Describe the <u>general pattern</u> and any <u>anomalies</u> (things that <u>don't fit</u> the general pattern).

3) Make <u>at least</u> as many <u>points</u> as there are <u>marks</u> and use <u>names</u> of places and <u>figures</u> if they're given.

4) If you're asked to give a <u>reason</u> or <u>explain</u>, you need to describe the <u>distribution</u> <u>first</u>.

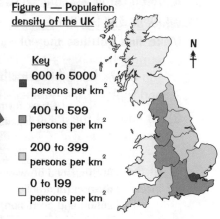

Figure 1 — Population density of the UK

Key
- 600 to 5000 persons per km²
- 400 to 599 persons per km²
- 200 to 399 persons per km²
- 0 to 199 persons per km²

Q: Use Figure 1 to explain the pattern of population density in the UK.

A: The <u>London area</u> has a <u>very high</u> population density (<u>600 to 5000</u> per km²). There are also areas of <u>high</u> population density (<u>400 to 599</u> per km²) in the <u>south east</u> and <u>west</u> of England. These areas include <u>major cities</u> (e.g. Birmingham and Manchester). More people live in and around cities because there are <u>better services</u> and <u>more job opportunities</u> than in rural areas. <u>Scotland</u> and <u>Wales</u> have the <u>lowest</u> population density in the UK (<u>less than 199</u> per km²)...

You could be given two maps to use for one question — link information from the two maps together.

Describing Locations <u>on Maps</u> — <u>Include Details</u>

1) In your exams you could get a question like, 'suggest a <u>reason</u> for the <u>location</u> of the mines'.

2) When you're asked about the <u>location</u> of something say <u>where</u> it is, what it's <u>near</u> and use <u>compass points</u>.

3) If you're asked to give a <u>reason</u> or <u>explain</u>, you need to describe the <u>location</u> <u>first</u>.

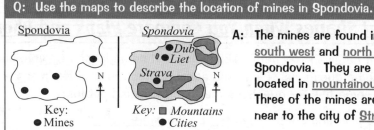

Q: Use the maps to describe the location of mines in Spondovia.

Spondovia

Key:
● Mines

Spondovia
● Dub
● Liet
Strava

Key: ☐ Mountains
● Cities

A: The mines are found in the <u>south west</u> and <u>north east</u> of Spondovia. They are all located in <u>mountainous</u> areas. Three of the mines are located near to the city of <u>Strava</u>.

Describing what Graphs Show — <u>Include Figures</u> <u>from the Graph</u>

When <u>describing</u> graphs make sure you mention:

1) The general pattern — when it's <u>going up</u> and <u>down</u>, and any <u>peaks</u> (highest bits) and <u>troughs</u> (lowest bits).

2) Any <u>anomalies</u> (odd results).

3) Specific <u>data points</u>.

Q: Use the graph to describe population change in Cheeseham.

A: The population halved between 1950 and 1960 from 40 thousand people to 20 thousand people. It then increased to 100 thousand by 1980, before falling slightly and staying steady at 90 thousand from 1990 to 2000.

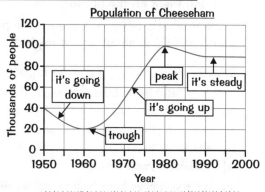

Population of Cheeseham

it's going down

peak   it's steady

it's going up

trough

If it's a scattergraph you can also talk about correlation — see page 100 for more.

Misfit data points with hats and fishing rods — a-gnome-alies...

Get it... a-gnome-alies.. I quite like gnomes, but then I also like studying <u>maps</u> and <u>graphs</u> just for kicks. I really should get out more, maybe I could go and visit the good people of Cheeseham... mmm... cheese.

Charts and Graphs

The next four pages are filled with lots of <u>different</u> types of <u>charts</u>, <u>graphs</u> and <u>maps</u>. There are two <u>important</u> things to learn — NUMBER ONE: how to <u>interpret</u> them (read them), and NUMBER TWO: how to <u>construct</u> and <u>complete</u> them (fill them in). You might have to do it in the <u>exam</u> so pay attention.

Bar Charts — Draw the Bars Straight and Neat

1) Reading Bar Charts

1) Read along the <u>bottom</u> to find the <u>bar</u> you want.

2) To find out the <u>value</u> of a bar in a <u>normal</u> bar chart — go from the <u>top</u> of the bar <u>across</u> to the <u>scale</u>, and <u>read off</u> the number.

3) To find out the <u>value</u> of <u>part</u> of the bar in a <u>divided</u> bar chart — find the <u>number at the top</u> of the part of the bar you're interested in, and <u>take away</u> the <u>number at the bottom</u> of it.

Q: How many barrels of oil did Oxo oil produce per day in 2008?

A: 500 thousand – 350 thousand = <u>150 thousand barrels</u> per day

Oil production
(bar chart showing 2007 and 2008 data for Oxo oil, Gnoxo Ltd., and Froxo Inc. — Thousands of barrels per day vs Company. "Line across from 350" dashed line)

2) Completing Bar Charts

1) First find the number you want on the <u>vertical scale</u>.

2) Then <u>trace</u> a line across to where you want the <u>top</u> of the bar to be with a <u>ruler</u>.

3) Draw in a bar of the <u>right size</u> using a <u>ruler</u>.

Q: Complete the chart to show that Froxo Inc. produced 200 thousand barrels of oil per day in 2008.

A: 150 thousand (2007) + 200 thousand = <u>350 thousand barrels</u>. So draw the bar up to this point.

Line Graphs — the Points are Joined by Lines

1) Reading Line Graphs

1) Read along the <u>correct scale</u> to find the <u>value</u> you want, e.g. 20 thousand tonnes or 1920.

2) Read <u>across</u> or <u>up</u> to the line you want, then read the value off the <u>other</u> scale.

Q: How much coal did New Wales Ltd. produce in 1900?

A: Find 1900 on the bottom scale, go up to the red line, read across, and it's 20 on the scale. The scale's in thousands of tonnes, so the answer is <u>20 thousand tonnes</u>.

Coal production
(line graph showing New Wales Ltd. and Old Wales Ltd. — Thousand tonnes vs Year, 1890–1930)

2) Completing Line Graphs

1) Find the value you want on <u>both scales</u>.

2) Make a <u>mark</u> (e.g. ✕) at the point where the <u>two values meet</u> on the graph.

3) Using a <u>ruler</u>, <u>join</u> the <u>mark</u> you've made to the <u>line</u> that it should be <u>connected to</u>.

Q: Complete the graph to show that Old Wales Ltd. produced 10 thousand tonnes of coal in 1930.

A: Find 1930 on the bottom scale, and 10 thousand tonnes on the vertical scale. Make a mark <u>where they meet</u>, then join it to the <u>blue</u> line <u>with a ruler</u>.

The top forty for sheep — the baaaaaaaaaaaaa chart...

Something to watch out for with <u>bar charts</u> and <u>line graphs</u> is reading the <u>scale</u> — check how much each division is <u>worth</u> before reading them or completing them. It's easy to think they're always worth one each, but sadly not.

Charts and Graphs

'More charts and graphs' I hear you cry — well OK, your weird wishes are my command.

Scatter Graphs Show Relationships

Scatter graphs tell you how closely related two things are, e.g. rainfall and river discharge. The fancy word for this is correlation. Strong correlation means the two things are closely related to each other. Weak correlation means they're not very closely related. The line of best fit is a line that goes roughly through the middle of the scatter of points and tells you about what type of correlation there is. Data can show three types of correlation:

1) Positive — as one thing increases the other increases.

2) Negative — as one thing increases the other decreases.

3) None — there's no relationship between the two things.

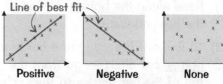

1 Reading Scatter Graphs

1) If you're asked to describe the relationship, look at the slope of the graph, e.g. if the line's moving upwards to the right it's a positive correlation. You also need to look at how close the points are to the line of best fit — the closer they are the stronger the correlation.

2) If you're asked to read off a specific point, just follow the rules for a line graph (see previous page).

Relationship between river discharge and rainfall

Q: Describe the relationship shown by the scatter graph.

A: River discharge and rainfall show a strong, positive correlation — as rainfall increases, so does river discharge.

2 Completing Scatter Graphs

1) You could be asked to draw a line of best fit — just draw it roughly through the middle of the scatter of points.

2) If you're asked to add a point — just follow the rules for adding a point to a line graph (see previous page).

Pie Charts Show Amounts or Percentages

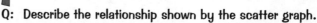

The important thing to remember with pie charts is that the whole pie = 360°.

1 Reading Pie Charts

1) To work out the % for a wedge of the pie, use a protractor to find out how large it is in degrees.

2) Then divide that number by 360 and times by 100.

3) To find the amount a wedge of the pie is worth, work out your percentage then turn it into a decimal. Then times the decimal by the total amount of the pie.

Pie Chart of Transport Type

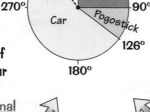

Q: Out of 100 people, how many used a pogostick?

A: 126 – 90 = 36°, so (36 ÷ 360) × 100 = 10%, so 0.1 × 100 = 10 people.

2 Completing Pie Charts

1) To draw on a new wedge that you know the % for, turn the % into a decimal and times it by 360. Then draw a wedge of that many degrees.

Q: Out of 100 people, 25% used a bicycle. Add this to the pie chart.

A: 25 ÷ 100 = 0.25, 0.25 × 360 = 90°.

2) To add a new wedge that you know the amount for, divide your amount by the total amount of the pie and times the answer by 360. Then draw on a wedge of that many degrees.

Q: Out of 100 people, 55 used a car, add this to the pie chart.

A: 55 ÷ 100 = 0.55, 0.55 × 360 = 198° (198° + 126° = 324°).

Sorry darling, we've got no relationship — look at our scatter graph...

Hmm, who'd have thought pie could be so complicated. Don't panic though, a bit of practice and you'll be fine. And don't worry, you're over half way through this section now. Congratulations — I'm so proud of you, sniff.

Maps

A couple of jazzy maps on this page for you, both with complicated names — <u>topological</u> and <u>proportional symbol</u>. And a bit on <u>isolines</u> too. Don't say I never treat you...

Topological Maps are Simplified Maps

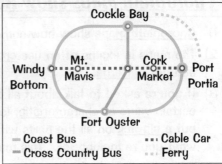

1) Some maps are <u>hard to read</u> because they show <u>too much detail</u>.

2) <u>Topological maps</u> get around this by just showing the <u>most important features</u> like <u>roads</u> and <u>rail lines</u>. They don't have <u>correct distances or directions</u> either, which makes them <u>easier to read</u>.

3) They're often used to show <u>transport networks</u>, e.g. the London tube map.

4) If you have to <u>read</u> a topological map — <u>dots</u> are usually <u>places</u> and <u>lines</u> usually show <u>routes</u> between places. If two lines cross <u>at a dot</u> then it's usually a place where you can <u>switch</u> routes.

5) As always, don't forget to check out the <u>key</u>.

Q: How many different transport routes pass through Port Portia?

A: Three (bus, cable car and ferry).

Proportional Symbol Maps use Symbols of Different Sizes

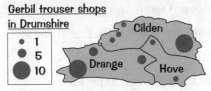

Gerbil trouser shops in Drumshire

● 1
● 5
● 10

Q: Which area of Drumshire has the most gerbil trouser shops?

A: Drange, with 20.

1) <u>Proportional symbol maps</u> use symbols of different <u>sizes</u> to represent different <u>quantities</u>.

2) A <u>key</u> shows the <u>quantity</u> each <u>different sized</u> symbol represents. The <u>bigger</u> the symbol, the <u>larger</u> the amount.

3) The symbols might be <u>circles</u>, <u>squares</u>, <u>semi-circles</u> or <u>bars</u>, but a <u>larger symbol</u> always means a <u>larger amount</u>.

Isolines on Maps Link up Places with Something in Common

1) <u>Isolines</u> are lines on a map <u>linking</u> up all the places where something's the <u>same</u>, for example:
   - <u>Contour lines</u> are isolines linking up places at the same <u>altitude</u> (height above sea level).
   - Isolines on a <u>weather map</u> (called <u>isobars</u>) link together all the places where the <u>pressure's</u> the same.

2) Isolines can be used to link up lots of things, e.g. <u>average temperature</u>, <u>wind speed</u> or <u>rainfall</u>.

① Reading Isoline Maps

1) <u>Find</u> the place you're interested in on the map and if it's on a <u>line</u> just <u>read</u> off the value.

2) If it's <u>between</u> two lines, you have to <u>estimate</u> the value.

Q: Find the altitude of Portia Park and Mavis Point.

A: Portia Park is about half way between the lines for 200 m and 400 m so its altitude is around 300 m above sea level. Mavis Point is on a contour line so it's 1000 m above sea level.

Altitude map of Itchy Island (metres above sea level)

② Completing Isoline Maps

1) Drawing an isoline's like doing a <u>dot-to-dot</u> — you just join up all the dots with the <u>same numbers</u>.

2) Make sure you don't <u>cross</u> any <u>other isolines</u> though.

Q: Complete on the map the contour line showing an altitude of 600 m.

A: See the red line on the map.

Lines and lines and lines...

If you have to draw an isoline on a map, then check all the info on the map <u>before</u> you start drawing. If you know where the line's got to go you won't <u>muck it up</u>. Make sure you do it in <u>pencil</u> too, so you can rub out any mistakes.

Maps

Three more maps, with three more ludicrous names. Well the last two aren't that bad, but this first one — <u>choropleth</u>, sounds like a treatment at the dentist.

Choropleth Maps show How Something Varies Between Different Areas

1) <u>Choropleth maps</u> show how something varies between different areas using <u>colours</u> or <u>patterns</u>.

2) The maps in exams often use <u>cross-hatched lines</u> and <u>dot patterns</u>.

3) If you're asked to talk about all the parts of the map with a certain <u>value</u> or <u>characteristic</u>, look at the map carefully and put a <u>big tick</u> on all the parts with the <u>pattern</u> that <u>matches</u> what you're looking for. This makes them all <u>stand out</u>.

4) When you're asked to <u>complete</u> part of a map, first use the <u>key</u> to work out what type of <u>pattern</u> you need. Then <u>carefully</u> draw on the pattern, e.g. using a <u>ruler</u>.

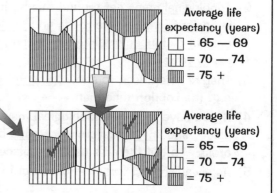

Average life expectancy (years)
☐ = 65 — 69
▥ = 70 — 74
▦ = 75 +

Average life expectancy (years)
☐ = 65 — 69
▥ = 70 — 74
▦ = 75 +

Flow Lines show Movement

1) <u>Flow line maps</u> have <u>arrows</u> on, showing how things <u>move</u> (or are moved) from one place to another.

2) They can also be <u>proportional symbol maps</u> — the <u>width</u> of the arrows show the <u>quantity</u> of things that are <u>moving</u>.

Q: From which <u>area</u> do the <u>greatest</u> number of people entering the UK come from?

A: <u>USA</u>, as this arrow is the largest.

Q: The number of people entering the UK from the <u>Middle East</u> is <u>roughly half</u> the number of people entering from the <u>USA</u>. Draw an <u>arrow</u> on the map to <u>show</u> this.

A: Make sure your arrow is going in the <u>right direction</u> and its <u>size</u> is appropriate (e.g. <u>half the width</u> of the USA arrow).

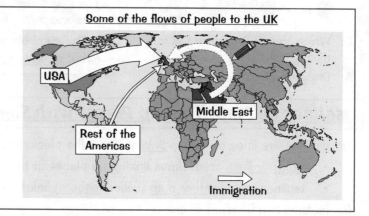

Some of the flows of people to the UK

USA

Middle East

Rest of the Americas

Immigration

Desire Lines show Journeys

1) <u>Desire line maps</u> are a type of flow line as they show <u>movement</u> too.

2) They're <u>straight lines</u> that show <u>journeys</u> <u>between</u> two <u>locations</u>, but they <u>don't follow</u> roads or railway lines.

3) <u>One line</u> represents <u>one journey</u>.

4) They're used to show <u>how far</u> all the people have <u>travelled</u> to get to a <u>place</u>, e.g. a shop or a town centre, and <u>where</u> they've <u>come from</u>.

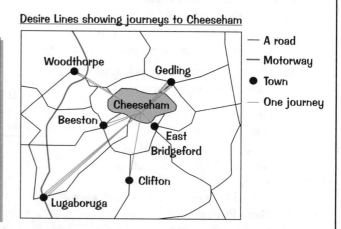

Desire Lines showing journeys to Cheeseham

— A road
— Motorway
● Town
— One journey

Woodthorpe
Gedling
Cheeseham
Beeston
East Bridgeford
Clifton
Lugaboruga

Desire lines — I'm sure my palm reader mentioned those...

...unfortunately I'm not as good at seeing the future as she is* so I can't predict if any of these <u>maps</u> are going to come up in your <u>exams</u>. They could do though, so make sure you know what they are and how to read them.

*If you're wondering, I'm going to meet a tall, dark, handsome stranger very soon....

Exam Skills

Ordnance Survey Maps

Next up, the dreaded Ordnance Survey® maps. Don't worry, they're easy once you know how to use 'em.

Learn These Common Symbols

Ordnance survey (OS®) maps use lots of symbols. It's a good idea to learn some of the most common ones — like these:

▬▬ Motorway	– · – County boundary
▬▬ Main (A) road	– – – National Park boundary
═══ Secondary (B) road	– – – – Footpath
⌒ Bridge	▢ Building
─── Railway	⬤ Bus station

PO Post Office®
PH Pub
+ Place of worship
⛏ Place of worship, with a tower
⛪ Church with a spire, minaret or dome

You have to be able to Understand Grid References

You need to be able to use four figure and six figure grid references for your exams.

Q: Give the four figure and six figure grid reference for the Post Office®.

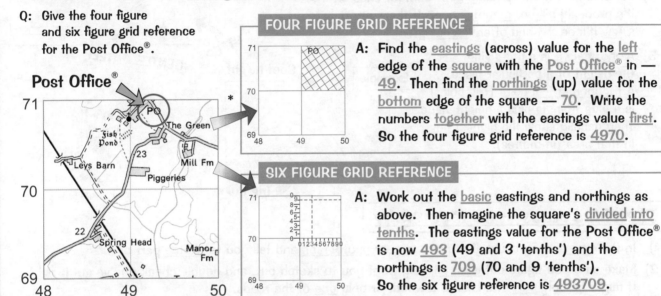

Post Office®

FOUR FIGURE GRID REFERENCE

A: Find the eastings (across) value for the left edge of the square with the Post Office® in — 49. Then find the northings (up) value for the bottom edge of the square — 70. Write the numbers together with the eastings value first. So the four figure grid reference is 4970.

SIX FIGURE GRID REFERENCE

A: Work out the basic eastings and northings as above. Then imagine the square's divided into tenths. The eastings value for the Post Office® is now 493 (49 and 3 'tenths') and the northings is 709 (70 and 9 'tenths'). So the six figure reference is 493709.

You need to Know your Compass Points

You've got to know the compass — for giving directions, saying which way a river's flowing, or knowing what they mean if they say 'look at the river in the NW of the map' in the exam. Read it out loud to yourself, going clockwise.

North
West — East
South

OR

Never
Wheat — Eat
Soggy

You Might have to Work Out the Distance Between Two Places

To work out the distance between two places on a map, use a ruler to measure the distance in cm then compare it to the scale to find the distance in km.

Q: What's the distance from the bridge (482703) to the church (490708)?

A: They're 2.2 cm apart on the map...

2.2 cm

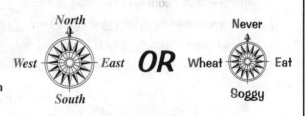

...which means they're 1.1 km apart in real life.

Scale 1:50 000
2 centimetres to 1 kilometre (one grid square)

1.1 km   Kilometres

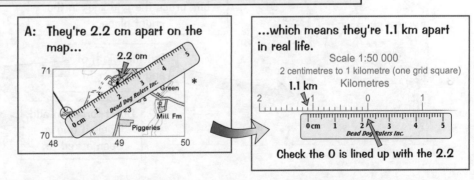

Check the 0 is lined up with the 2.2

Keeping ramblers happy since 1791...

I told you OS maps aren't as bad as you thought. If a dodgy looking rambler who's been walking in the rain for five hours with only a cup of tea to keep him going can read them, then so can you. Get ready for some more map fun...

* Maps: Reproduced from Ordnance Survey digital map data © Crown copyright 2001

Exam Skills

Ordnance Survey Maps

Almost done with <u>exam skills</u> now. Just this final page looking at <u>contour lines</u> and <u>sketching</u> from Ordnance Survey® maps or photographs to deal with then you're free, free I tell you...

The Relief of an Area is Shown by Contours and Spot Heights

1) <u>Contour lines</u> are the <u>orange lines</u> drawn on maps — they join points of <u>equal height</u> above sea level (<u>altitude</u>).

2) They tell you about the <u>relief</u> of the land, e.g. whether it's hilly, flat or steep.

3) They show the <u>height</u> of the land by the <u>numbers</u> marked on them. They also show the <u>steepness</u> of the land by how <u>close together</u> they are (the <u>closer</u> they are, the <u>steeper</u> the slope).

4) For example, if a map has <u>lots</u> of contour lines on it, it's probably <u>hilly</u> or <u>mountainous</u>. If there are only a <u>few</u> it'll be <u>flat</u> and often <u>low-lying</u>.

5) A <u>spot height</u> is a <u>dot</u> giving the height of a particular place. A <u>trigonometrical point</u> (trig point) is a <u>blue triangle</u> plus a height value. They usually show the <u>highest point</u> in that area (in metres).

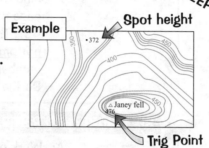

A contour map of the Mona Lisa

Sketching Maps — Do it Carefully

1) In the <u>exams</u>, they could give you a <u>map</u> or <u>photograph</u> and tell you to <u>sketch</u> part of it.

2) Make sure you figure out <u>what bit</u> they want you to sketch out, and <u>double check</u> you've <u>got it right</u>. It might be only <u>part</u> of a lake or a wood, or only <u>one</u> of the roads.

3) If you're <u>sketching</u> an <u>OS</u>® map, it's a good idea to <u>copy</u> the <u>grid</u> from the map onto your sketch paper — this helps you to copy the map <u>accurately</u>.

4) Draw your sketch <u>in pencil</u> so you can <u>rub it out</u> if it's <u>wrong</u>.

5) Look at how much <u>time</u> you have and <u>how many marks</u> it's worth to decide how much <u>detail</u> to add.

Q: Draw a labelled sketch of the OS map shown below.

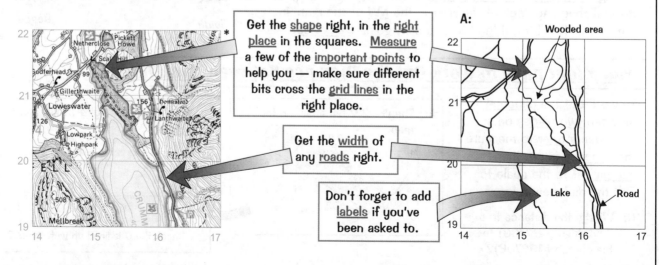

Get the <u>shape</u> right, in the <u>right place</u> in the squares. <u>Measure</u> a few of the <u>important points</u> to help you — make sure different bits cross the <u>grid lines</u> in the right place.

Get the <u>width</u> of any <u>roads</u> right.

Don't forget to add <u>labels</u> if you've been asked to.

What a relief that's over...

When you're <u>sketching</u> a copy of a map or photo see if you can lay the paper over it — then you can <u>trace</u> it (sneaky). And that my friends is the <u>end of the book</u>. Now go treat yourself to some exams.

Index

Index

Index

Index